# COMPUTER-AIDED GRAPHICS AND DESIGN

## COMPUTER-AIDED ENGINEERING

Series Editor

### Mark E. Coticchia

Carnegie Mellon University
Pittsburgh, Pennsylvania

1. Integrated Computer Network Systems, *Frank Welch*
2. CAD/CAM/CAE Systems: Justification · Implementation · Productivity Measurement, Second Edition, Revised and Expanded, *Mark E. Coticchia, George W. Crawford, and Edward J. Preston*
3. Computer Graphics for CAD/CAM Systems, *Jack E. Zecher*
4. Computer-Aided Graphics and Design, Third Edition, Revised and Expanded, *Daniel L. Ryan*

**ADDITIONAL VOLUMES IN PREPARATION**

Methods and Tools for Applied Artificial Intelligence, *Dobrivoje Popovic and Vijay Bhatkar*

# COMPUTER-AIDED GRAPHICS AND DESIGN

## THIRD EDITION, REVISED AND EXPANDED

**DANIEL L. RYAN**

*Clemson University*
*Clemson, South Carolina*

CRC Press
Taylor & Francis Group
Boca Raton  London  New York

CRC Press is an imprint of the
Taylor & Francis Group, an **informa** business

First published 1994 by Marcel Dekker, Inc.

Published 2021 by CRC Press
Taylor & Francis Group
6000 Broken Sound Parkway NW, Suite 300
Boca Raton, FL 33487-2742

© 1994 by Taylor & Francis Group, LLC
CRC Press is an imprint of Taylor & Francis Group, an Informa business

No claim to original U.S. Government works

ISBN 13: 978-0-8247-9164-3 (hbk)

**Visit the Taylor & Francis Web site at**
**http://www.taylorandfrancis.com**

**and the CRC Press Web site at**
**http://www.crcpress.com**

**Library of Congress Cataloging-in-Publication Data**

Ryan, Daniel L.
  Computer-aided graphics and design / Daniel L. Ryan. — 3rd ed.,
rev. and expanded.
    p.  cm. — (Computer-aided engineering)
  Includes index.
  ISBN 0-8247-9164-9
  1. Computer graphics. 2. Computer-aided design. I. Title.
II. Series: Computer-aided engineering (New York, N.Y.)
T385.R9 1994
006.6—dc20
                                   93-46012
                                       CIP

# Series Introduction

The Computer-Aided Engineering series represents a commitment by Marcel Dekker, Inc., to develop a book program with the goal of providing the most current information in a form easily accessible to practitioners, educators, and students. Titles in the series include works focused on specific technologies, as well as more comprehensive texts and reference books. All titles will present fundamental principles along with the latest methodologies.

The term computer-aided engineering (CAE) has widespread meaning throughout engineering disciplines as well as for this series. The series encompasses all computer-based applications used in design, manufacturing, and analysis. Various computer platforms, hardware configurations, and software programs are addressed, along with the trends, industries, and state-of-the-art applications. The overriding emphasis is on the use of computer technology as related to current engineering processes, methods, and tools.

Computer-aided engineering is a science and technology of great significance and is fundamental to total quality. It generally is faster, less expensive, and more precise than the conventional "test and build" approach. CAE provides commercial organizations with a competitive advantage, resulting in less product development time and cost and offering alternatives that could not be considered in the past. Considering the competitiveness in which engineering operates in day's world, business without this technology will not survive in the long term.

Mark E. Coticchia

# Preface

This third edition reflects the many changes that have been requested by the thousands of readers who have used the first edition (1979) and the second edition (1985) of this classic approach to computer-automated graphics and design instruction. The theory of presentation has remained the same—that is, the beginning level has not changed—but the applications and illustrations have all been updated to reflect readers' requests for a wide range of hardware platforms (graphic workstations from many different manufacturers) that will run a single set of software options from Autodesk, Inc. These options include AutoCAD 12.0, AutoSketch 3.0, Generic CADD 6.0, AutoConvert, AutoShade, AutoSolid, GenCADD, Generic 3D, Symbol Libraries, Multimedia Explorer, HOME series, Chaos, and CA Lab.

This edition has evolved from a 1991 series of lecture notes that were used to present several seminars in this multihardware, single software vendor format. These seminars were presented on a national and international basis, ranging from ASEE national presentations to presentations in the People's Republic of China. Much of the material in this edition has also been student-tested at Clemson University. It is hoped, therefore, that all errors, ambiguities, and confusing explanations have been corrected.

*Computer-Aided Graphics and Design* is tailored for a three-semester-hour course. For shorter courses or seminars, the chapters dealing with language-dependent applications (AutoLISP) may be omitted without destroying the continuity of the text. The selection of material in this text is based on the premise that the reader has had a course in computer languages (FORTRAN, used in the first two editions, has been replaced by LISP). Therefore, many basic situations are included without lengthy explanations or solutions. This makes it possible to keep the emphasis on CADD applications, not programming. Methods of using existing Autodesk software are stressed, as is the procedure for writing new ones in LISP. The emphasis, however, is on the use rather than the creation. It is the author's belief that this delimitation is necessary in a first course in CADD, because programming requires more ingenuity, inventiveness, imagination, and patience. An ability to create new software functions can best be developed by experience after the basic CADD techniques are well understood.

The unique features of this book include coverage of the following applications:

1. Design and drafting—using Autodesk's product line
2. Business graphics/multimedia—to help engineers produce top-notch graphics with sight and sound
3. Home computing—for residential planning and landscaping
4. Science—to show microstructures and animated graphics on screen
5. Education—as a manual or desktop tutorial.

Although the book draws heavily on products developed by Autodesk, Inc., it remains a pioneer effort in the techniques of simulating methods heretofore confined to the laboratory. The unique character of this book lies in its industrial orientation: the sequencing of the topics discussed and the documentary and user-oriented manner in which they are presented.

A number of leading industrial organizations generously assisted the author by supplying appropriate photographs needed in developing the topics. The author deeply appreciates the kindness and generosity of those companies and the personnel who found the time to consult and to allow the author to visit their various manufacturing plants.

Not to be forgotten are the many persons—some students and some teachers—who have made valuable contributions to this classroom text. The author's indebtedness to excellent, intelligent students is hereby reaffirmed.

Daniel L. Ryan

# Contents

# COMPUTER-AIDED GRAPHICS AND DESIGN

# 1

# Introduction to CADD

A complete study of engineering graphics must include something about the age of computerization and how it affects work done by an engineer or technician. The human being is smart, creative, and slow, whereas the computer is stupid, uncreative, but never tires. The problem, then, is to allow the person and the computer to work well together as a team to control the CADD (computer-aided drafting and design) functions. The graphics workstation is such an example of human–computer control. Certainly, the simulation of human—computer characteristics complement each other, but their languages are very different. We think in symbols and pictures, whereas the computer understands only simple electrical impulses. CADD is playing an increasingly large part in our daily work lives. Over the past decade, CADD applications have been justified because they can save money and time and can improve the quality of the drafting product. Dollar savings of from 3:1 to 6:1, and time savings of from 20:1 to 50:1, are typical of those quoted in applications explained later in this book.

CADD is a way of converting computer impulses into engineering documents and, conversely, to translate the operator's instructions into electronic data. In many of the more sophisticated systems, we need know little about computer programming to control the CADD effect.

## 1.1  Quality of CADD Documents

Most CADD devices are easy-to-operate, self-contained computer systems for the direct translation of rough sketches into high-quality finished documents. The systems are designed for simple, real-time operation by technicians or engineers and are particularly useful for producing drawings containing repetitive symbology and text. The first example that comes to mind is the desktop personal computer or laptop computer. These types of computers can be used as graphic workstations since they do not depend on an outside processing source. So if you have such a computer, you will not need to spend money upgrading your existing equipment. The same goes for printers and plotters. From 85 pen plotters to over 300 dot-matrix, laser, PostScript, and color printers, CADD offers the same high-quality, finished look for your printed or plotted drawings as that shown in Figure 1.1. A powerful CADD software package does not have to be expensive to satisfy your drafting needs. With inexpensive CADD you'll find a two-dimensional computer-aided design and drafting tool that is as at home with initial sketches and conceptual designs as it is with final-presentation drawings and full-scale engineering or architecture projects. Whether you create electrical schematics, assembly drawings, or architectural floor plans, CADD offers you a way to get the needed document. That is why it continues to win such industry praise and why so many design and engineering professionals use CADD.

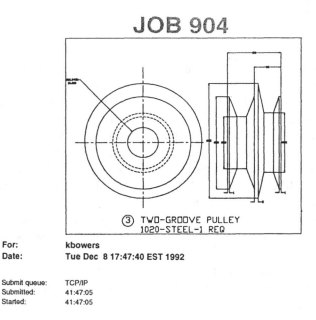

**Figure 1.1**  Typical CADD output. (Courtesy DLR Associates.)

Many of the illustrations, diagrams, and photoenhancements used in this book were produced as computer displays with the aid and instructions of a human computer. A CADD document, then, is a combination of two or more elements to produce synergy, or united action. The logical basis for this concept lies in the fact that the human mind tends to solve problems heuristically (by trial and error), whereas a CADD system solves by the use of algorithms (an error-free sequence of logic). By letting each mind/machine work to its best capacity, a new and better method can be automated. How this human–machine process is automated is rather simple. Strictly speaking, the automation of any process means the improvement or elimination of certain or all parts of the manual labor involved in doing a job. This does not mean the elimination of human beings from the scene, for we have to start and stop the process, either directly by pushing a button or indirectly by programming another machine device, such as a computer. For example, modern graphics workstations can be programmed so that all the data in a computer file can be displayed by pressing a single function key. The signal of the depressed key releases a set of data points that can describe an entire document or something as simple as a fastener.

The first automatic drafting machines to come onto the market, called *X-Y plotters,* eliminated the need for a design engineer to push and pull a triangle and T-square around a drafting table. The first step toward CADD was the elimination of outmoded, single-tasked plotters. The design engineer is still there to operate a CADD operation much as was done before. But now the plotter is only one of several input–output (I/O) operations available with the same central processing unit (CPU). A good example of these types of CPUs are those presently in use in the personal computer industry.

## 1.2 Definition of Terms

Graphic workstations are playing an increasingly large part in engineering efforts. After some initial problems, we have learned to work with them. To many of us, a computer is a genie that can produce monumental results, either technically wonderful or technically fouled up. Our uneasiness is due largely to a basic lack of understanding of what a computer can and cannot do. Used improperly, almost any mistake can be blamed on the computer. To gain acceptance, some products are labeled "computer designed" when in fact the design of the product had nothing to do with a computer. Also, when we know too little about a computer, we do not protest when a badly thought-out feature of a computer-designed system subjects us to inconvenience.

Unfortunately, a person who tries to learn more about computers quickly encounters a problem. A language full of colorful terms has evolved with computers. Slang, technical terms, and phrases used by computer manufacturers all contribute to the problem. To the graphics workstation operator, it is a natural medium for expressing ideas, but to the uninitiated it is a puzzle to be solved. To help solve the puzzle, the author offers the lengthly glossary presented as Table 1.1. Fortunately, understanding what graphic workstations are all about does not require more than ordinary language. With Table 1.1 as a starting point, graphic workstations can be categorized by the software used (see Table 1.2).

**Table 1.1**   Glossary of Computer-Aided Drafting and Design

| Term | Definition |
| --- | --- |
| APERTURE | Controls the size of the object snap target box |
| ARC | Draws an arc of any size |
| AREA | Finds a polygon's area and perimeter |
| ARRAY | Makes multiple copies of selected objects in a rectangular or circular pattern |
| ATTDEF | Creates an attribute definition entity for textual information to be associated with a block definition |
| ATTDISP | Controls the visibility of attribute entities on a global basis |
| ATTEDIT | Permits editing of attributes |
| ATTEXT | Extracts attribute data from a drawing |
| AXIS | Displays a "ruler line" on the graphics monitor |
| BASE | Specifies origin for subsequent insertion into another drawing |
| BLIPMODE | Controls display of marker blips for point selection |
| BLOCK | Forms a compound objct from a group of entities |
| BREAK | Erases part of an object, or splits it into two objects |
| CHAMFER | Creates a chamfer at the intersection of two lines |
| CHANGE | Alters the location, size, or orientation of selected objects; especially useful for text entities |
| CIRCLE | Draws a circle of any size |
| COLOR | Establishes the color for objects drawn subsequently |
| COPY | Draws a copy of selected objects |
| DBLIST | Lists database information for every entity in a drawing |
| DELAY | Delays, for a specified time, execution of the next command |
| DIM | Invokes dimensioning mode, permitting many dimension notations to be added to a drawing |
| DIM1 | Allows one dimension notation to be added to a drawing, then returns to normal command mode |
| DIST | Finds the distance between two points |
| DIVIDE | Places markers along an object, dividing it into a specified number of equal parts |
| DONUT | *Same as* DOUGHNUT |
| DOUGHNUT | Draws rings with specified inside and outside diameters |
| DRAGMODE | Allows control of the dynamic specification ("dragging") feature for all appropriate commands |
| DTEXT | Draws text items dynamically |
| DXBIN | Inserts specially coded binary files into a drawing; special-purpose command for programs such as CAD/camera |
| DXFIN | Loads a drawing interchange file |
| DXFOUT | Write a drawing interchange file |
| ELEV | Sets elevation and extrusion thickness for subsequently drawn entities; used in three-dimensional visualizations |
| ELLIPSE | Draws ellipses using any of several specifications |
| END | Exits the drawing editor after saving the updated drawing |
| ERASE | Erases entities from the drawing |
| EXPLODE | Shatters a block or polyline to meet another object |
| FILES | Performs disk file utility tasks |
| FILL | Controls whether solids, traces, and wide polylines are automatically filled on the screen and the plot output |

**Table 1.1** (continued)

| Term | Definition |
| --- | --- |
| FILLET | Constructs a smooth arc of specified radius between two lines, arcs, or circles |
| 'GRAPHSCR | Flips to the graphics display on single-screen systems; used in command scripts and menus |
| GRID | Displays a grid of dots, at the desired spacing, on the screen |
| HATCH | Performs crosshatching and pattern filling |
| 'HELP or '? | Displays a list of valid commands and data-entry options or obtains help for a specific command |
| HIDE | Regenerates a three-dimensional visualization with "hidden" lines removed |
| ID | Displays the coordinates of a specified point |
| IGESIN | Loads an IGES interchange file |
| IGESOUT | Writes an IGES interchange file |
| INSERT | Inserts a copy of a previously drawn part (object) into the current drawing |
| ISOPLANE | Selects the plane of an isometric grid to be the "current" plane for orthogonal drawing |
| LAYER | Creates named drawing layers and assigns color and linetype properties to those layers |
| LIMITS | Changes the drawing boundaries and controls checking of those boundaries |
| LINE | Draws straight lines of any length |
| LINETYPE | Defines linetypes (sequences of alternating line segments and spaces), loads them from libraries, and sets the linetype for subsequently drawn objects |
| LIST | Lists database information for selected objects |
| LOAD | Loads a file of user-defined shapes to be used with the SHAPE command |
| LTSCALE | Specifies a scaling factor to be applied to all linetypes within the drawing |
| MEASURE | Places markers at specified intervals along an object |
| MENU | Loads a file of drawing editor commands into the menu areas (screen, tablet, and button) |
| MINSERT | Inserts multiple copies of a block in a rectangular pattern |
| MIRROR | Reflects designated entities about a user-specified axis |
| MOVE | Moves designated entities to another location |
| MSLIDE | Makes a slide file from the current display |
| OFFSET | Allows the creation of offset curves and parallel lines |
| OOPS | Restores erased entities |
| ORTHO | Constrains LINE drawing so that only lines aligned with the current grid can be entered |
| OSNAP | Enables points to be precisely located on reference points of existing objects |
| PAN | Moves the display window |
| PEDIT | Permits editing of polylines |
| PLINE | Draws connected line and arc segments, with optional width and taper |
| PLOT | Plots a drawing on a pen plotter |
| POINT | Draws single points |
| POLYGON | Draws regular polygons with the specified number of sides |
| PRPLOT | Plots a drawing on a printer plotter |
| PURGE | Removes unused blocks, text styles, layers, or linetypes from the drawing |
| QTEXT | Enables text entities to be identified without drawing the text detail |
| QUIT | Exits the drawing editor and returns to AutoCAD's main menu, discarding any changes to the drawing |
| REDO | Reverse the previous command if it was U or UNDO |

**Table 1.1**   (continued)

| Term | Definition |
| --- | --- |
| REDRAW | Refreshes or cleans up the display |
| REGEN | Regenerates the entire drawing |
| REGENAUTO | Allows control of automatic drawing regeneration performed by other commands |
| RENAME | Changes the names associated with text styles, named views, layers, linetypes, and blocks |
| 'RESUME | Resumes an interrupted command script |
| ROTATE | Rotates existing objects |
| RSCRIPT | Restarts a command script from the beginning |
| SAVE | Updates the current drawing file without exiting the drawing editor |
| SCALE | Alters the size of existing objects |
| SCRIPT | Executes a command script |
| SELECT | Groups objects into a selection set for use in subsequent commands |
| 'SETVAR | Allows the user to display or change the value of system variables |
| SH | On MS-DOS/PC-DOS systems, allows access to internal DOS commands |
| SHAPE | Draws predefined shapes |
| SHELL | Allows access to other programs while running AutoCAD |
| SKETCH | Permits freehand sketching |
| SNAP | Specifies a "round-off" interval for digitizer point entry so that entities can easily be placed at precise locations |
| SOLID | Draws filled-in polygons |
| STATUS | Displays statistics about the current drawing |
| STRETCH | Allows the user to move a portion of a drawing while retaining connections to other parts of the drawing |
| STYLE | Creates named text styles, with user-selected combinations of font, mirroring, obliquing, and horizontal scaling |
| TABLET | Aligns the digitizing tablet with coordinates of a paper drawing to copy it accurately with AutoCAD |
| TEXT | Draws text characters of any size with styles selected |
| 'TEXTSCR | Flips to the text display on single-screen systems; used in command scripts and menus |
| TIME | Displays drawing creation and update times, and permits control of an elapsed timer |
| TRACE | Draws solid lines of specified width |
| TRIM | Erases the portions of selected entities that cross a specified boundary |
| U | Reverses the effect of the preceding command |
| UNDO | Reverses the effect of multiple commands and provides control over the "undo" facility |
| UNITS | Selects coordinate and angle display formats and precision |
| VIEW | Saves the current graphics display as a named view, or restores a saved view to the display |
| VIEWRES | Allows the use to control the precision and speed of cirle and arc drawing on the monitor by specifying the number of sides in a cirle |
| VPOINT | Selects the viewpoint for a three-dimensional visualization |
| VSLIDE | Displays a previously created slide file |
| WBLOCK | Writes selected entities to a disk file |
| ZOOM | Enlarges or reduces the display of the drawing |

**Table 1.2** CADD Software Listing

| Name | Compatible with this book? |
|---|---|
| AutoCAD | Yes |
| AutoConvert | Yes |
| AutoSketch | Yes |
| CADKEY | No |
| CADVance | No |
| CA Lab | Yes |
| Chaos | Yes |
| Data CADD | No |
| Drafix | No |
| Design Board | No |
| EE Designer | No |
| GenCADD | Yes |
| Generic CADD | Yes |
| Home | Yes |
| MicroCAD | No |
| Multimedia | Yes |
| P-CAD | No |
| ProDesign | No |
| RoboCAD | No |
| VersaCAD | No |

## 1.3 Types of Equipment

In this section we can select items from Tables 1.3 to 1.6 to make a complete workstation. These specifications are necessary to work the exercises presented at the ends of subsequent chapters. To use a workstation you must obtain as a minimum the hardware items illustrated in Figure 1.2: system unit, display monitor, keyboard, and printer or plotter. The system should contain:

1. A 1-megabyte random-access read/write memory
2. Two diskette drives (A and B)
3. Disk controller board and hard disk (C)
4. Eight I/O expansion slots
5. Serial/parallel adapter board
6. Battery-backed real-time clock and CMOS system configuration
7. Dual-speed processor board for 386- or 486-based software
8. Video display tube (VDT) selected from Table 1.4
9. Math coprocessor to run software selected from Table 1.2
10. Operating system selected from Table 1.5

In most cases these components will arrive from the manufacturer in shipping cartons. Open the system unit carton first and follow the steps shown on the shipping attachment. Remove the packing material and dust covers carefully. Place the system unit on a flat surface large enough to hold all the other pieces of hardware. Next, unpack

**Table 1.3** Current CADD Equipment Manufacturers

| Manufacturer | Type of device |
| --- | --- |
| ADI | Digitizer, plotter, printer |
| Alpha Merics | Plotter |
| Amdek | Plotter |
| AMT | Printer |
| Apple Macintosh | CPU |
| AT&T | CPU |
| CALCOMP | Tablets, plotters |
| Compaq | CPU |
| Cordata | Laser printer |
| Datacopy | Printer |
| DISC Instruments | Track ball |
| Eagle | CPU |
| Epson | Printers, CPU |
| Geographics | Tablet |
| Gould | Plotters |
| GTLO | Digitizer |
| Hewlett-Packard | Mouse, digitizer, plotter (laser jet), CPU |
| Hitachi | Tablet |
| Houston Instruments | Tablet, plotter |
| IBM | Plotter, printer, CPU |
| Imagen | Plotter |
| Ioline | Plotter |
| ITT | CPU |
| JDL | Printer |
| Kaypro | CPU |
| Kola | Digipad |
| Kurta | Tablet |
| Leading edge | CPU |
| Logitech | Mouse |
| Microsoft | Mouse |
| Mitsubishi | Printer |
| Mouse Systems | Mouse |
| Mutoh | Digitizer |
| NEL | CPU |
| Nicolet | Plotter |
| Numonics | Tablet |
| Okidata | Printer |
| Olivetti | CPU |
| Pencept | Digitizer |
| Penman | Plotter |
| PostScript | Printer/plotter |
| Printronix | Printer |
| Roland | Plotter |
| SAC | Digitizer |
| Scriptel | Tablet |

**Table 1.3** (continued)

| Manufacturer | Type of device |
|---|---|
| Seiko | Tablet |
| Sperry | CPU |
| Summagraphics | Tablet, mouse |
| Sweet-P | Plotter |
| Tandy | CPU |
| Texas Instruments | Printer/plotter, CPU |
| Torrington | Mouse |
| Toshiba | CPU |
| Watanabe | Plotter |
| Wyse | CPU |
| Zenith | CPU |

**Table 1.4** Video Display Tube Options for Autodesk Software

| Display device | Maximum number of colors | Maximum resolution | Configuration |
|---|---|---|---|
| BNW Graphics Adapter | 16 | 1024 × 1024 | Dual screen |
| Cambridge Micro-1024 | Monochrome | 1024 × 780 | Dual screen |
| Conographic Model 40 | 16 | 640 × 400 | Single screen |
| Control Systems ARTIST I | 16 | 1024 × 1024 | Dual screen |
| Control Systems ARTIST II | 16 | 640 × 400 | Dual screen |
| Control Systems Transformer | 16 | 640 × 400 | Single screen |
| Cordata FastDraft 480 | 16 | 640 × 480 | Single or dual screen |
| Frontier CADgraph2 | 16 | 640 × 480 | Dual screen |
| GraphAx 20/20 Graphics Card | 16 | 2048 × 1280 | Dual screen |
| Hercules Graphics Card | Monochrome | 720 × 348 | Single screen |
| Hewlett Packard EGA | 16 | 640 × 350 | Single screen |
| | 16 | 640 × 200 | Single screen |
| | Monochrome | 640 × 350 | Single screen |
| Hewlett-Packard Multi Mode | Monochrome | 640 × 400 | Single screen |
| Hewlett-Packard 82960 | 256 | 640 × 480 | Single or dual screen |
| IBM Professional Graphics | 256 | 640 × 480 | Single or dual screen |
| Matrox PG-640 | 256 | 640 × 480 | Single or dual screen |
| Metheus Omega | 16 | 1024 × 768 | Single screen |
| Micro-Display Genius | Monochrome | 728 × 1004 | Single screen |
| Number 9 NNIOS Board | 16 | 1024 × 768 | Dual screen |
| Number 9 Revolution Board | 256 | 512 × 512 | Dual screen |
| Persyst BOB-16 | 16 | 640 × 400 | Single screen |
| Profit Systems Multigraph I | Monochrome | 968 × 512 | Single or dual screen |
| Quadram Quadscreen | Monochrome | 968 × 512 | Single or dual screen |
| Quintar GraphPort | 16 | 832 × 630 | Dual screen |
| | 16 | 640 × 480 | Dual screen |
| Quintar Model 1080 | 16 | 640 × 480 | Dual screen |
| Ramtek | 16 | 1280 × 1024 | Dual screen |
| Sigma Designs Color 400 | 16 | 640 × 400 | Single screen |
| STB Chauffer | Monochrome | 640 × 352 | Single screen |

**Table 1.4** (continued)

| Display device | Maximum number of colors | Maximum resolution | Configuration |
|---|---|---|---|
| STB Super Res 400 | 16 | 320 × 400 | Dual screen |
| STB XVI | 16 | 320 × 200 | Single or dual screen |
| TAT Galaxy G-500 | 16 | 1024 × 768 | Dual screen |
| Tecmar Graphics Master | 16 | 640 × 400 | Single screen |
| Vectrix Midas Card Set | 256 | 640 × 480 | Dual screen |
| Vectrix PEPE | 16 | 1024 × 1024 | Dual screen |
| Vectrix VX384 | 256 | 672 × 512 | Dual screen |
| Vermont (VMI 1024) | 256 | 1024 × 800 | Single or dual screen |
| Verticom M16 | 16 | 640 × 480 | Single or dual screen |
| Verticom H16 | 16 | 1024 × 768 | Single or dual screen |
| Wyse Technology WY-700 | Monochrome | 1280 × 800 | Single or dual screen |

**Table 1.5** Graphic Workstation Operating Systems

| Supplier | Limitations |
|---|---|
| AEGIS | None |
| Apple | Macintosh II |
| IBM | PC-DOS, OS/2 |
| Microsoft | MS-DOS |
| UNIX | None |
| VMS | None |

**Table 1.6** Graphic Software from Autodesk, Inc.

| Name | Extensions |
|---|---|
| AutoCAD 12.0 | AutoLISP, AutoSOLID, AutoShade, AutoFlix |
| AutoConvert | None |
| AutoSketch 3.0 | Symbols |
| CA Lab | Symbols |
| Chaos | None |
| GenCADD | Architectural/Civil |
| Generic CADD | 6.0, Apple Macintosh |
| Home | Kitchen, Bath, Landscape |
| Multimedia | Explorer |

**Figure 1.2** Typical CADD graphics workstation. (Courtesy DLR Associates.)

**Figure 1.3**   Installing the graphics workstation. (Courtesy DLR Associates.)

the keyboard (Figure 1.3) and place it in front of the system unit. Do not try to attach cables at this point. Continuing to open cartons, unpack the display unit and place it directly on top of the system unit. Finally, open the carton and unpack the plotter or printer. Your workstation has now arrived and you have carefully unpacked the hardware items and arranged them as pictured in Figure 1.3. You are now ready to interconnect and test the workstation.

## 1.4  Workstation Installation

Begin the installation process with the system unit. Connect the monitor and keyboard to the rear of the system unit as shown in Figure 1.4. First, make sure that the system unit power switch is off as indicated in the assembly instructions. Next, connect the system unit power cord to the unit, then to the wall outlet.

You are now ready to test the monitor and keyboard installation. Turn on the system unit power switch. You should hear one short beep after the memory is checked. This will take between 13 and 90 seconds, depending on the amount of memory or-

**Figure 1.4**   Testing the graphics workstation. (Courtesy DLR Associates.)

dered. It is also normal to hear diskette drive motor noise and see the "in use" light on for a short time. If you heard one short beep, your workstation has completed its self-test. If you hear nothing or anything other than the short beep and the diskette drive, return your workstation to the manufacturer for adjustment.

You are now ready to install the plotter or printer. Refer again to the rear of the system unit. Plug the printer into the printer connection port (note that additional wall outlet power is needed). You are now ready to test the graphic workstation.

## 1.5   Testing the Workstation

Each of the components can be adjusted for your operational comfort. For example, the keyboard has adjustable tilt positions, and the display monitor has various adjustments. Stop now and adjust the keyboard for typing comfort and the monitor for eye comfort. The monitor and printer should be powered-on before the system unit power is turned on. Now power-on the system unit. You will notice that there are now three responses:

A cursor appears on the monitor screen in approximately 4 seconds, the short beep will be heard after the memory is tested, and a message is printed.

You are now ready to test the system. Locate the diagnostics diskette. Turn the system unit power switch off. Lift the diskette drive A load lever and insert the diagnostics diskette. Be sure to push the diskette in until it stops. Now push the load lever down so that it will latch closed. Turn the system unit power switch on.

If you are using an IBM-compatible display with your workstation and the information on the screen is shifted to the left or right, press function key F8 to move the information to the right, or function key F7 to move the information to the left. Center the information by using the function keys to match the following display:

```
THE GRAPHIC WORKSTATION DIAGNOSTICS
VERSION XXX (C) COPYRIGHT XXXX,XXXX

0 - RUN DIAGNOSTIC ROUTINES
1 - FORMAT DISKETTE
2 - COPY TO DISKETTE
3 - PREPARE SYSTEM FOR RELOCATION
9 - EXIT TO SYSTEM DISKETTE

INSERT DIAGNOSTIC DISKETTE IN DRIVE
A AND ENTER THE ACTION DESIRED
```

## 1.6  Diagnostic Routines

During the diagnostic tests you will need a second diskette. We shall select option 0 from the listing above, so after the ? prompt, type the 0 character and press the enter key. Your display monitor should now look as follows

```
THE INSTALLED DEVICES ARE

S   SYSTEM BOARD
S   1 MB MEMORY
S   KEYBOARD
S   COLOR/GRAPHICS MONITOR ADAPTER
S   2 DISKETTE DRIVE(S) AND ADAPTOR
S   ASYNC COMMUNICATIONS ADAPTOR

IS THE LIST CORRECT (Y/N)?
```

You will note that the printer (or plotter) was not turned on for this test and was not listed. Type a Y and press the enter key. Your display monitor will now match this:

```
SYSTEM CHECKOUT

0 - RUN TESTS ONE TIME
1 - RUN TESTS MULTIPLE TIMES
```

```
2 - LOG UTILITIES
9 - EXIT DIAGNOSTICS ROUTINES

ENTER THE ACTION DESIRED

?
```

Select the 0 option, type it, and enter it. Your display monitor will now read

```
SYSTEM UNIT    100
THIS TEST TAKES UP TO TWO MINUTES
PLEASE STAND BY
```

After approximately 2 minutes, your screen will go blank, SYSTEM UNIT 200 will appear on the monitor for an instant, and then the screen will look as follows:

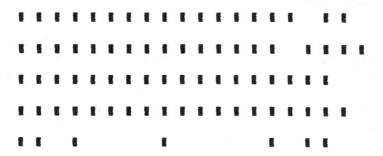

```
PRESS EACH KEY, HOLD FOR TYPEMATIC TEST
IF OK PRESS "Y ENTER"
IF NOT OK PRESS "N ENTER"
```

## 1.7  CADD from AutoLISP

Finding an easy way to use a CADD program suitable for your specific design needs can be a time-consuming process. Engineering design is broad based and covers many possible combinations of the traditional engineering fields. The only intelligent solution is the tailormade CADD packages that you produce for yourself. The CADD language introduced in this chapter is AutoLISP. It is an implementation of the LISP programming language embedded in Autodesk when you purchase that software for use with the graphic workstation. This allows you to tailormake CADD functions in a very powerful high-level language that is well suited for use later in this book. In addition, LISP is easy to learn and use on the workstation. You will find yourself adapting it to many design problem situations.

The remainder of this chapter is a reference guide with teaching examples—it is not a LISP programming tutorial. So don't worry, it is not necessary to learn programming to make effective use of Autodesk software. If you have no experience in computer programming, you should still learn how to develop CADD functions without difficulty. If you enjoy programming, however, you should not only grasp the simple teaching exercises, but also develop entire programs for many different types of design problems. If you are already using MacLISP, InterLISP, ZetaLISP, or common LISP, you will find that AutoLISP adheres closely to these.

LISP supports several different data types. They are:

1. Lists
2. Symbols
3. Strings
4. Real numbers
5. Integers
6. File descriptors
7. Autodesk entity names
8. Autodesk selection sets
9. subrs (functions)

Lists, symbols, and strings are all part of teaching examples used later in this chapter. Integers are 16-bit signed numbers; therefore, their range is between –32,768 and +32,767. Real numbers are represented as double-precision floating point. Strings can be of any length because for them, memory is dynamically allocated.

At the heart of every LISP interpreter is the evaluator. The evaluator takes a line of user input, evaluates it, and returns a result. This process is fundamental to engineering design analysis. The following is the process of evaluation in LISP:

1. Integers, reals, strings, file pointers, and subrs evaluate themselves.
2. Symbols evaluate to the value of their current binding.
3. Lists are evaluated according to the first element of the list.

If you enter a LISP expression in response to Autodesk's `Command:`, LISP evaluates the expression and prints its result. `Command:` then reappears. If an incorrect expression is type or read from a file, LISP will display

    n>

where n is an integer showing how many levels of left parentheses remain unclosed. You may then correct the error.

LISP input can take several forms. It can be typed from a keyboard within Autodesk, and read from a file or string variable. The conventions are as follows:

1. Symbol names can consist of any sequence of characters except

    ( ) . ' " ;

2. Symbol, function names, or subrs are not case sensitive but must not start with a digit.
3. Integer constants may begin with an optional + or – character.
4. Real constants consist of one or more digits followed by a decimal point.

5. Literal strings are surrounded by " . Text control characters may be entered by a backslash followed by

> means the character
>
> e means escape
>
> n means new line
>
> r means return
>
> nn means the character whose octal code is nn

6. A single quote can be used as shorthand for the QUOTE function: 'box is equivalent to (quote box).

7. Comments can be included in LISP programs. They begion with a semicolon:

```
; This is a comment line
```

## 1.8  LISP Notation

Throughout the remainder of this chapter, AutoLISP notation is used to document the behavior of functions. For example:

```
(box <string> <number> ...)
```

where the function name is BOX, and the angle-bracketed (<  >) items indicate the types of function arguments needed. In this case the function BOX has two required arguments (inputs): a literal string and a number. The ellipsis (...) indicates that additional numbers may be supplied to the function. Do not include angle brackets when entering an AutoLISP statement: they are used for notation (explanation) only.

In a teaching example, suppose that the BOX were a square:

```
(BOX "SQUARE" 5)
```

would be a valid use of the AutoLISP statement because a square has equal-length sides, in this case 5 units. Suppose that the BOX were a rectangle:

```
(BOX "RECTANGLE" 5 8)
```

would also be a valid use. The following example statements are not valid:

```
(BOX 5 8)      First argument must be a string.
(BOX "SQUARE")      Missing data/number argument.
(BOX "TRAPEZOID" (4 8 7 2))      Second argument must be a number,
    not a list.
```

When an optional argument may appear once but cannot be repeated, the argument will be enclosed in square brackets ([1]), as follows:

```
(circle <string> [ <number>]
```

In this case the function CIRCLE requires one string input, such as ARC, and accepts one numeric argument, say 7, which is the only radius the arc could have.

## 1.9 Automatic LISP Functions

AutoLISP is supplied with the Autodesk software; no special installation is required. The file ACAD.OVL in the software release is the overlay file. Another of the files is called README.DOC and when listed should provide additional information. Each time an Autodesk design session begins, AutoLISP loads the file ACAD.LSP. You may add tailormade design functions to this file and they will be evaluated automatically each time you begin a design analysis session.

## 1.10 The ACAD.LSP File

AutoLISP provides numerous predefined design functions. Each design function is called by giving its name (upper or lower case) as the first element, with the arguments to that function as the subsequent arguments. Following is an alphabetic listing of all the AutoLISP design functions.

1. (ABS <number>) This function returns the absolute value of <n>. N may be a real number of an integer; for example,

(ABS 100) returns 100

2. (AND <expr> ....) This will return the logical AND of a list of expressions. It returns false if any of the expressions evaluate as false or unknown; otherwise, it returns true. If we had the LISP function sequence

```
(setq a 4)
(setq b "square")
(setq c "rectangle")
(setq d 8)
```

then

```
(and BOX b a) returns true.
(and BOX c a d) returns true.
(and a b c d e) returns false.
```

3. (ANGLE <pt1> <pt 2>) This function returns the angle in radians between two real points; for example,

(angle '(5. 1.33) '(2.4 1.33)) returns 3.141593.

4. (ANGTOS <angle> [ <mode> [ <precision>]] ) This function takes ANGLE and returns it as degrees, degrees–minutes–seconds, grads, radians, or surveyor's units. For example, if we had

```
(setq pt1 '(5. 1.33))
(setq pt2 '(2.4 1.33))
(setq a (angle pt1 pt2))
```

then

```
(angtos a 0 0)  returns 180 degrees.
(angtos a 0 4)  returns 180.0000 degrees.
(angtos a 1 4)  returns 180d0'0''.
(angtos a 3 4)  returns 3.1416.
(angtos a 4 2)  returns W.
```

5.   (APPEND <expr> ....)   This function takes any number of expressions and runs them together as one list. For example,

```
(append '(a b) '(c d))  returns (A B C D).
```

6.   (APPLY <function> <list>)   This executes the function with the arguments in the list. APPLY works with automatic functions or with any tailormade design functions that you might add to the ACAD.LSP file. For example,

```
(apply '+(123))  returns 6.
```

7.   (ARITHMETIC <number> ....)   The functions (+ - * / = /= < <= > >= _ 1+ 1- atan cos exp expt fix float gcd log lsh max min pi polar sin sqrt) return the sum, subtraction, product, dividend, equal to, not equal to, less than, less than or equal to, greater than, greater than or equal to, bitwise not, number increased by 1, number reduced by 1, arctanent, cosine, exponential (e or base), integer, real, greatest common denominator, natural log, integer, justification, maximum or minimum value, 3.1415926, coordinates, sine, and square root.

8.   (ASCII <string>)   This function returns the conversion of the first character of a string into it ASCII character code. This is similar to the ASC function in BASIC and has two subtypes: ATOF (returns string into a rael) and ATOI (returns string into an integer).

9.   (BOOLE <func> <int1> <int2> ....)   This is a bitwise boolean function where func is an integer between 0 and 15 which represents one of the 16 possible boolean functions in two variables (int1 and int2). See the boolean function AND at the beginning of the list. Others are ATOM, BOUNDP, COND, EVAL, EQ or EQUAL, FOREACH, IF, NOR, NOT, NULL, NUMBERP, OR, VER, XOR, and ZEROP.

10.   (CHR <number>)   Similar to the CHR$ function in BASIC, this function returns the conversion of an integer representing an ASCII character code into a single-character string. For example,

```
(chr 97>  returns "a".
```

11.   (COMMAND <args> ....)   This function executes Autodesk commands from within LISP. For example,

```
(setq pt1 '(1.4 3.2))
(set pt2 '(4.8 6.4))
(command "line" pt1 pt2)  displays a line between point 1 and point 2.
```

12. (DEFUN <sym> [ <argument list> <expr>1....) This automatic function is used to create a new function called sym with or without an argument list and with or without an expression. Be careful to select useful names for your tailormade functions and do not select the name of an automatic LISP function, as this will destroy (replace) the AutoLISP function. For example,

```
(defun add 10 (x) (+10x)) returns ADD10.
(add10 10) returns 20.
(add 10 -7) returns 3.
```

You can add new commands to Autodesk software by using DEFUN to define these functions implementing Autodesk commands. To be used as an Autodesk command later in this book, the function must have a name starting with C: and any three letters desired as long as the name does not duplicate another Autodesk command. For example,

```
(defun C:BOX(pt1 pt2 pt3 pt4 len)
(setq pt1 (getpoint "lower left corner of box:"))
(setq len (getdist pt1 "Length of one side:2))
(set pt2 (polar pt1 0.0 len))
(setq pt3 (polar pt2 (/pi 2.0) len))
(setq pt4 (polar pt3 pi len))
(command "PLINE" pt1 pt2 pt3 pt4 "C"))
```

13. (DISTANCE <pt1> <pt>) This function returns the distance between the two points. For example,

```
(distance '(1. 2.5) '(7.7 2.5)) returns 6.7.
```

14. (GET ....) This function pauses for user input and has several subtypes: angle, dist, int, point, real, string, and var. For example,

```
(setq ang (getangle '(1. 3.5))
```

15. (INTERS <pt1> <pt2> <pt3> <pt4> [<onseg>]) This function examines the two lines defined by points 1,2 and 3,4 and then returns the point of intersection on the line segment. For example,

```
(setq a '(1. 1.) b '(9. 9.) c '(4. 1.) d '(4. 2.))
(inters a b c d nil) returns (4.4).
```

16. (LAMBDA <arguments> <expr> ....) This is a "dummy" function used when a designer is laying out a function at the spot where it is to be used. See item 21 for an example.

17. (LAST <list>) This function returns the last element in a list. For example,

```
<last '(a b c d)) returns d.
```

18. (LENGTH <list>) This function returns the total number of elements in the list. In the example above, the total number in the list is 4.

19. (LIST <expr> ....)  This function takes any number of expressions and strings them together to form a list. For example,

```
(list 'a 'b 3.9 '(b c) 6.7)
```

20. (LOAD <filename>)  This function is used to load a file of automatic LISP expressions and evaluate those expressions. The "Filename.lsp" may include a directory prefix. On DOS a drive letter is also permitted and you can use the back-slash method of hard-disk instruction.

21. (MAPCAR <function> <list> ....)  This returns the result of executing the function with the individual elements of a list supplied as arguments to the function. For example,

```
(MAPCAR '1+ '(10 20 30)) returns (11 21 31).
(MAPCAR 7 (LAMBDA(xyz)(** (-yz))where 7(5 6) '(20 30) '(14
   5.0) returns (30 150.).
```

22. (MEMBER <expr> <list>)  This searches the list for an occurrence of the expression and returns the remainder of the list starting with the first occurrence of the expression. An alternative use of this function might be

```
(NTH <n> <list>)
```

Here the "nth" element of the list is returned, where **n** is the locator.

23. (OPEN <filename> <mode>)  This function opens a file for access by LISP and is used as follows:

```
(setq a (open "file.ext" "r"))
```

Using this and the automatic LISP function CLOSE, other files may be opened and closed at the discretion of the designer.

24. (PROGN <expr> ....)  This function evaluates each expression sequentially and returns the value of the last expression. For example,

```
(if (=a b) (progn (set a (+a 10) b (-b 10))))
```

The IF normally evaluates one THEN expression, but in this case we have used PROGN to cause to expressions to be evaluated.

25. (PROMPT <msg>)  This will display any message on the screen's prompt area. For example,

```
(prompt "Set new values:")
```

26. (QUOTE <expr>)  simply returns the expression unevaluated. For example,

```
'C=A+B
```

27. (READ ....)  This function has three types: READ <string>, READ-CHAR [<file-desc>], and READ-LINE [<file-desc>]. For example,

```
(read "hello, Fred") returns hello, Fred.
(read-char) waits for a keyboard character.
(read-line f)
```

28. (REPEAT ....) Three functions—repeat, reverse, and rtos—are used:

```
(repeat <number> <expr> ....)
(reverse <list>)
(rtos <number> [ <mode> [ <precision>]])
```

29. (SET ....) Three versions of SET are used:

```
(set <sym> <expr>)
(setq <sym> <expr> ....)
(setvar <var> <value>)
```

30. (STR ....) Three string functions can be used:

```
(STRCASE <string> [ <which>])
(STRCAT <string> <string 2> ....)
(STRLEN <string>)
```

Each takes a string specified and returns a copy of all alphabetic characters converted to upper or lower case, depending on the arguments.

31. (SUBST <newitem> <old item> <list>) This searches a list for an old item and returns a copy of the list with the new item substituted in place of every old item. If the entire string is to be replaced, (SUBSTR <string> <start> [ <length>]).

32. (TRACE <function> ....) This function is used to debug an AutoLISP program. It searches for the function specified and returns the last function name. To clear the debug (trace) function, use (untrace <function>).

33. (WRITE ....) Two types of writes can be used, write-char and write-line. These functions write to the screen or to an open file described by

```
(write-char <num> [ <file-desc>])
(write-line <string> [ <file-desc>])
```

## 1.11 Automatic LISP Features

Much of the power of CADD comes from the ability to customize it for the user. Although software such as Autodesk puts some power in your hands, it is doubtful that

```
File to list <ACAD>:

Linetypes defined in file C:\ACAD

Name            Description
------------    --------------------
DASHED          __  __  __  __  __  __  __  __  __  __  __  __  __
HIDDEN          _ _ _ _ _ _ _ _ _ _ _ _ _ _ _ _ _ _ _ _ _ _ _ _ _
CENTER          ____  _  ____  _  ____  _  ____  _  ____  _  ____  _
PHANTOM         ____  _  _  ____  _  _  ____  _  _  ____  _  _  ____
DOT             ...............................................

DASHDOT         __  .  __  .  __  .  __  .  __  .  __  .  __  .  __  .  __  .
BORDER          __  __  .  __  __  .  __  __  .  __  __  .  __  __  .  __  __
DIVIDE          __  .  .  __  .  .  __  .  .  __  .  .  __  .  .  __

?/Create/Load/Set:
```

**Figure 1.5** Common CADD linetypes.

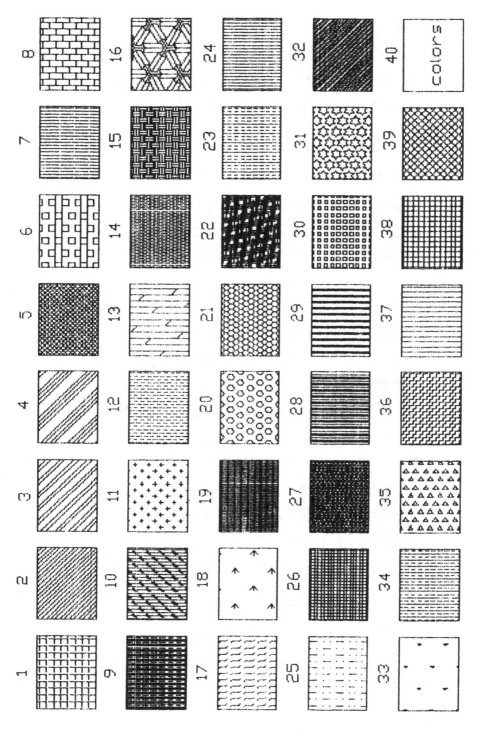

**Figure 1.6** Typical CADD hatch patterns.

!"#$%&'()*+,-./01234567
89:;<=>?@ABCDEFGHIJKLMNO
PQRSTUVWXYZ[\]^_`abcdefg
hijklmnopqrstuvwxyz{|}~°±ø

TXT font

---

!"#$%&'()*+,-./01234567
89:;<=>?@ABCDEFGHIJKLMNO
PQRSTUVWXYZ[\]^_`abcdefg
hijklmnopqrstuvwxyz{|}~°±ø

SIMPLEX font

---

!"#$%&'()*+,-./01234567
89:;<=>?@ABCDEFGHIJKLMNO
PQRSTUVWXYZ[\]^_`abcdefg
hijklmnopqrstuvwxyz{|}~°±ø

COMPLEX font

---

!"#$%&'()*+,-./01234567
89:;<=>?@ABCDEFGHIJKLMNO
PQRSTUVWXYZ[\]^_`abcdefg
hijklmnopqrstuvwxyz{|}~°±ø

ITALIC font

**Figure 1.7**  Typical CADD text fonts.

any software company will include all the features that you require as a designer. As you use this book and the Autodesk software purchased with it, you may find that you would like to have a capability that you need on repeated occasions. You may start out adding sequences of commands to the screen, buttons, or tablet menu. You may define linetypes as shown in Figure 1.5, hatch patterns as shown in Figure 1.6, or even different text fonts as shown in Figure 1.7. As you do this you are taking advantage of the techniques described throughout this book. You will develop your own personal design tool, responsive to the way you think and work. In the next section we add a new command to the Autodesk software. In the process you will see how the automatic LISP commands described earlier work for you. The new command we develop is oriented to engineering mechanics (fasteners), but the concepts are relevant regardless of the application area.

## 1.12  Command Syntax

We will develop a new command for Autodesk that displays a rectangular gusset plate. As the plate must be lightweight, it will incorporate several holes designed to reduce weight while maximizing strength. Our new command will have the following prompt syntax:

Command PLATE
Start point of plate: start point

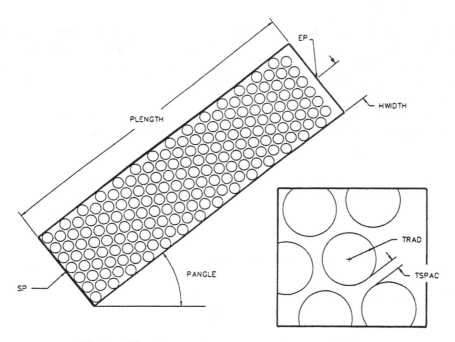

**Figure 1.8**  Output of new CADD command PLATE.

End point of plate: end point
Half width of plate: number
Radius of holes: number
Spacing between holes: number

where the start point (sp) and end point (ep) specify the centerline of the plate, as indicated in Figure 1.8. Because of the centerline approach, only the half-width of the plate is required, but if the width itself would be easier to work with, you can input the width and then halve it inside the design function. Similarly, the radius is required, but the hole diameter may be somewhat easier to remember. Finally, the spacing between holes is specified.

## 1.13  Writing Design Functions

We will write this design function as most are written, from the inside out or bottom up. We are required to use an angle to place the gusset plate as shown in Figure 1.8. LISP specifies angles in radians. Radians measure angles from zero to $2\pi$. Since most designers think in angles of degrees, we define a function that converts degrees to radians. Using a line editor from the workstation manual, we create a file called GP.LSP. Enter it as shown in Figure 1.9. Let us consider what the program does. The first line is a comment, and the second defines a function, using DEFUN, called DTR (degrees to radians). It takes one argument "a", the angle in degrees. Its result is the expression

```
PI * (a/180.0)
```

The second step in writing the design function is to ask the user where to display the plate, how wide to make it, the size of the holes, and how closely to space them. Using the editor, add lines to GP.LSP as shown in Figure 1.10. Notice that here we have created another function, called GPU (gusset plate user), which takes no arguments and asks the user to supply the information needed.

The third step in the design function is to display its outline. Add to the GP.LSP file the lines indicated in Figure 1.11. This addition defines a function, called DRW,

```
;  Convert degrees to radians

(defun dtr (a)
     (*pi (/a 180.0))
)
```

**Figure 1.9**  LISP programming segment 1.

```
;  Convert degrees to radians

(defun dtr (a)
     (*pi (/a 180.0))
 )


;  Acquire information for gusset plate

 (defun gpu ()
        (setq sp (getpoint " nstart point of plate!"))`
        (setq ep (getpoint " nend point of plate! "))
        (setq hwidth (getdist " nhalf width of plate!" sp))
        (setq trad (getdist " nradius of holes!" sp))
        (setq tspac (getdist " nspacing between holes!" " sp))
        (setq pangle (angle sp ep))
        (setq plength (distance sp ep))
        (setq width (*2 hwidth))
        (setq angp90 (+ pangle (dtr 90)))   ; Path angle +90 degrees
        (setq angm90 (- pangle (dtr 90)))   ; Path angle -90 degrees
```

**Figure 1.10**   LISP programming segment 2.

```
    ;  Draw outline of plate

    (defun drw ()
         (command "pline"
           (setq p (polar sp angm90 hwidth))
           (setq p (polar p pangle plength)
           (setq p (polar p angp90 width)
           (polar p (+ pangle (dtr 180)) plength)
           "close"
          )
    )
```

**Figure 1.11**   LISP programming segment 3.

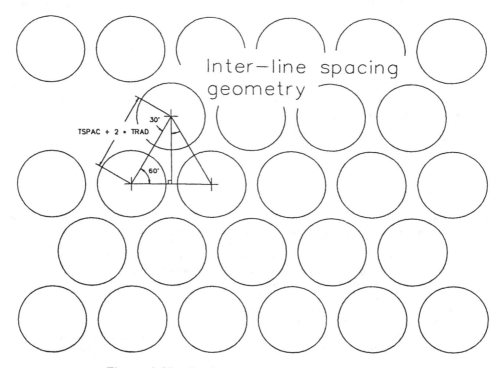

**Figure 1.12** Spacing technique for PLATE command.

```
;  Place one row of holes given distance along plate

(defun drh (pd offset)
    (setq pfirst (polar sp pangle pd))
    (setq pchole (polar pfirst angp90 offset))
    (setq plhole pchole)
    (while (<(distance pfirst plhole) (-hwidth trad))
        (command "circle" plhole trad)
        (setq plhole (polar plhole angp90 (+tspac trad trad)))
    )
)

;  Draw all the rows

(defun drr ()
    (setq pdist (+ trad tspac))
    (setq off 0.0)
    (while (<= pdist (- plength trad))
        (drh pdist off)
        (setq pdist (+ pdist  (*(+  tspac  trad  trad) (sin (dtr
60)))))
        (if (= off 0.0)
           (setq off (* (+ tspac trad trad) (cos (dtr 60))))
           (setq off 0.0)
        )
    )
)
```

**Figure 1.13** LISP programming segment 4.

which uses the starting point, angle, and length of the plate obtained by GPU and draws an outline of the plate. The plate outline is drawn by an Autodesk routine known as polyline (pline). The DRW function submits data to Autodesk software for display. All of the other functions were described earlier. For example, each corner of the plate is located by using the POLAR function, stored in the variable P.

The fourth and final step is addition of the holes in the gusset plate. To do this we will be doing some geometric design, as shown in Figure 1.12. Using Figure 1.12, add to GP.LSP the lines shown in Figure 1.13. To understand the operation of these functions, compare Figures 1.8 and 1.12. The function DRH (draw hole) draws a row of holes at a given distance along the plate as specified in the argument. We want to offset the holes in alternate rows to decrease weight and increase strength. We test GP.LSP in Chapter 10.

## 1.14   Adding GP.LSP to Autodesk

When new design functions are written and tested, they may be added to any Autodesk software package by using

```
C:PLATE
```

To do this we define a closing function with the editor for GP.LSP as shown in Figure 1.14. The entire rile GP.LSP should look like Figure 1.15. As our plate design package executes inside Autodesk software, all the commands it submits will be echoed to the command/prompt area, and all the points it selects will be flagged on the screen with small crosses (blips). Once PLATE is debugged, this output may be turned off to make the LISP-generated graphics appear exactly like the commands covered. Add the lines indicated in Figure 1.16 to GP.LSP to suppress command echoing and blips.

```
;   Execute command, calling constituent functions

(defun C:PLATE ()
      (dtr)
      (gpu)
      (drw)
      (drh)
      (drr)
)
```

**Figure 1.14**   LISP programming closing function.

```
;  Convert degrees to radians
(defun dtr (a)
    (*pi (/a 180.0))
 )
;  Acquire information for gusset plate
 (defun gpu ()
      (setq sp (getpoint " nstart point of plate:"))
      (setq ep (getpoint " nend point of plate: "))
      (setq hwidth (getdist " nhalf width of plate:" sp))
      (setq trad (getdist " nradius of holes:" sp))
      (setq tspac (getdist " nspacing between holes:" " sp))
      (setq pangle (angle sp ep))
      (setq plength (distance sp ep))
      (setq width (*2 hwidth))
      (setq angp90 (+ pangle (dtr 90)))   ; Path angle +90 degrees
      (setq angm90 (- pangle (dtr 90)))   ; Path angle -90 degrees
)
;   Draw outline of plate
(defun drw ()
    (command "pline"
       (setq p (polar sp angm90 hwidth))
       (setq p (polar p pangle plength))
       (setq p (polar p angp90 width)
       (polar p (+ pangle (dtr 180)) plength)
       "close"
       )
)
;  Place one row of holes given distance along plate
(defun drh (pd offset)
    (setq pfirst (polar sp pangle pd))
    (setq pchole (polar pfirst angp90 offset))
    (setq plhole pchole)
    (while (((distance pfirst plhole) (-hwidth trad))
       (command "circle" plhole trad)
       (setq plhole (polar plhole angp90 (+tspac trad trad)))
       )
)
;  Draw all the rows
(defun drr ()
    (setq pdist (+ trad tspac))
    (setq off 0.0)
    (while ((<= pdist (- plength trad))
       (drh pdist off)
       (setq pdist (+ pdist (*(+ tspac trad trad) (sin (dtr 60)))))
       (if (= off 0.0)
          (setq off (* (+ tspac trad trad) (cos (dtr 60))))
          (setq off 0.0)
          )
       )
)
;  Execute command, calling constituent functions
(defun C:PLATE ()
    (dtr)
    (gpu)


    (drw)
    (drh)
    (drr)
)
```

**Figure 1.15**   Entire LISP listing.

```
;  Execute command, calling AutoDesk commands

(defun C:PLATE ()
      (dtr)
      (gpu)
      (setq sblip (getvar "blipmode"))
      (setq scmde (getvar "cmdecho"))
      (setvar "blipmode" 0)
      (setvar "cmdecho" 0)
      (drw)
      (drh)
      (setvar "blipmode" sblip)
      (setvar "cmdecho" scmde)
)
```

**Figure 1.16**  Suppress command echoing and blips.

## Exercises

1.  Begin a course notebook divided into the following sections: (A) classroom notse, (B) operational instructions for graphic workstation, (C) sample set of LISP instructions, and (D) sample outputs from a graphic workstation.

2.  From your local computing center, obtain handouts for section B in Exercise 1. Read each pamphlet or manual and incorporate index tabs for easy location of each section. Subdivide section B so that each CADD device can be described separately.

3.  Prepare a sample set of installation instructions for each of the items in Figure 2.3.

4.  Save the screen outputs of an example graphics dump as shown in Figure 1.1.

5.  Select from Table 1.3 or 1.4 a current CADD manufacturer with which you are not familiar. Locate the proper mailing address in the *Thomas Register* and prepare a business letter requesting up-to-date operational information. Include the response in your notebook.

6.  Write a short description of equipment based on the materials received upon completion of Exercise 5.

7.  Input the LISP programming segments shown in Figures 1.9 and 1.10.

8.  Input the LISP programming segments shown in Figures 1.11 to 1.13.

9.  Input the LISP programming segments shown in Figures 1.14 to 1.16.

10. Prepare a section in your notebook called "new terms" in which you list all terms that are new to you that do not appear in Table 1.1.

# 2
# Principles of CADD

Computer-aided graphics (CADD) is a fundamental form of engineering graphics. The concept is applicable to any kind of display that must be done in manufacturing. Methods for doing this are not new; as early as 1807 a 6-inch paper tape was used to control textile loom needles for sewing monograms or labels in many different graphic shapes and colors. Other early forerunners were used in the printing and machine tool industries, where the concept was used to etch patterns for tracing template work.

The engineering profession was slower in its use of CADD. In the early 1950s, the U.S. military used an interactive CRT graphic system called SAGE. In this system the controller pointed at a target or aircraft with a light pen, and the computer immediately presented information regarding that target. In the early 1960s, in a different environment, the TX-1 computer at the Massachusetts Institute of Technology featured a graphics console similar to that of SAGE. About 25 years ago, General Motors began to apply computer graphics to computer-generated design drawings. One of the milestones in the development of CADD was the work done by Ivan Sutherland, whose 1963 MIT doctoral thesis describing Sketch-Pad contains some of the data structures that laid the theoretical basis for CADD.

In the mid-1960s, large aerospace companies such as Lockheed, McDonnel Douglas, Ryan, and Boeing began to explore the use of CADD for aircraft and missile design. Uniformly, they reported dollar and time savings. At the same time, other industries, including Motorola, Fairchild, and Bell Laboratories, began to use CADD for the design and production of robots for automated manufacturing. The 1980s saw a rapid increase in the use of CADD in the design of robotic functions and manufacturing techniques, including computer display and computer-aided manufacturing instructions for machine tool operations. As a result of this work, most N/C (numerically controlled) machines are now obsolete. The use of CADD by design engineers to produce output control began about 30 years ago. From this beginning, the field of CADD has grown until today every major industry has some sort of CADD capability.

## 2.1 Line Segments

A CADD workstation accepts symbolic values from a processor [a central processing unit (CPU)] and converts this input into physical values through electrical signals that are translated into VDT (video display tube) line segments. These signals are usually digital pulses, but analog varying voltages can also be used (refer to Table 1.4 for further information on VDT types).

There are two major types of digital signals. One supplies incremental data and reports how much VDT beam display has occurred. In other words, each line display begins with a zero reading and ends with the distance traveled. The second type of digital signal is absolute. In this case each pulse signal corresponds to a specific location on the VDT. More than one line segment in a sequence is added end to end, or the last display of the VDT beam shows the total distance traveled since display began. Both methods are used by CADD manufacturers, some of whom allow either method to be used on the same workstation. In this case the operator selects the type of graphic output that is better for the type of data being generated from the processing unit.

Regardless of the method used to output a line segment, most applications require the generation of line motion. This type of movement usually can be achieved easily and quickly by a suitable programmed LISP routine. These routines produce display commands that define the desired beam location and the image base that describes what the line segment looks like. Remember, a function is what the CPU does (straight-line segment); a routine contains LISP instructions for what appears on the display screen. LISP routines inside the CADD software used in conjunction with this book are called device drivers by Autodesk, Inc. Remember, it is the device driver that enables the VDT to produce movable line segments. An example of a LISP-written routine is shown in Figure 2.1.

When unique CADD graphics requirements cannot be satisfied using existing LISP routines, the designer can write special-purpose AutoLISP routines that provide direct control of line segments and the generation of graphic shapes as shown in Chapter 1. By using the routines shown in the present chapter, however, the designer can do 90 percent of the display work. The LISP routine is stored as LINSEG. The LINSEG routine is used primarily to move the VDT beam in a straight line to a new position. It converts the designer's data to the appropriate sequence of display images.

```
;***************** LINSEG () ********************
;
;   Function to handle a line segment of a polyline
;
(defun linseg()
    (setq maxrad (- (car cenx) (cadr (assoc 10 v1list))))
    (setq minrad (- (car cenx) (ccadr(assoc 10 v2list))))
    (setq h (- (cadr (assoc 10 v2list))
               (cadr (assoc 10 v1list))
          )
    )
    (desg)
    (command "array" (entlast) "" "P" cen segno array-deg "")
    (setq elev (+ elev h))
; reset the elevation for next segment
)
```

**Figure 2.1**   Example of LISP routine.

The calling sequence has the following operation:

```
Command: LINSEG (S,E)
```

where S is the start point and E is the end point of the straight-line segment, and LINSEG is the representation of line motion. The file for Figure 2.1 is loaded from an AutoDesk device driver as shown in Chapter 1.

## 2.2  Angles and Optimal Moves

Any software system that accepts a numerical value as an input and converts it to a physical value (such as the display of an object) and its movement as an output is providing CADD format. Whether the distances (S,E) are put into the system using a keyboard, mouse, light pen, or joystick, and whether or not the system requires feedback, are secondary functions that are not part of the basic CADD concept.

The particular type of CADD display function is under the control of the designer, and if not part of the input commands, may perform as many as eight functions:

1. Select the line type called for.
2. Set the origin or "home" position.
3. Select the LISP routines (straight, optimal circular).
4. Activate the AutoDesk functions.
5. Load the device drivers required.
6. Start and stop the drawing files.
7. Use the mouse, joystick, and menu items.
8. Save the drawing files on external storage, as shown in Figure 2.2.

The basic concept of the LISP routine has been explained only insofar as point-to-point line segments were concerned. If a combination line (horizontal as well as vertical) is fed from the workstation, the VDT will produce that line also.

**Figure 2.2**  Disk drive for workstation. (Courtesy DLR Associates.)

## 2.3  Other LISP Routines

A complete set of LISP routines can now be loaded into the workstation for testing. Use the device shown in Figure 2.2 and a current copy of Autodesk's AutoSketch. The material for this chapter is based on the AutoSketch licensing agreement with Autodesk, Inc., 2320 Marinship Way, Sausalito, CA 94965. The software package that you purchase is protected by U.S. and international copyright law, so you must act as a first-party user. In other words, you must agree not to rent or lease the software in any form. Read the AutoSketch licensing agreement that accompanies your purchase, sign the agreement form, and return to Autodesk, Inc., which retains all title to the software and all diagrams used in the instruction manual.

## 2.4  Software Description

AutoSketch is a product for CADD users. Using this software approach, a new user can gain experience without drowning in a sea of CADD commands and options. It is extremely easy to use, yet offers many design features found previously only in software costing several thousand dollars. This is important, because the emphasis in this chapter is on basic principles, not on learning how a graphics system works.

Just as word processors have changed the ease and speed with which reports are written, AutoSketch is beginning to change how designers gather information. Using this approach you can create clean, precise images, and revise notes and drawings without having to redraw. You will be able to use common forms and shapes, duplicate these automatically, and make instant copies of base drawing and detailed notes. The procedure is totally compatible with techniques introduced in subsequent chapters.

## 2.5   Installing the Software

In this section we present installation procedures and tests to get you sketching right away. Before you start, remember to make a copy of the AutoSketch diskettes. Use DISCOPY from the operating system selected in Chapter 1, storing the original in a safe place and using the backup as the working copy. Installation is very easy. Simply place the copy in the device shown in Figure 2.2 To run, type

```
SKETCH <enter>
```

at the DOS A>.
    If you have a hard disk (C>:), place your working copy in the drive and enter

```
MD SKETCH<enter>
CD SKETCH<enter>
COPY A:*.*<enter>
```

and the installation is complete.
    When you want to run from disk C>: type

```
CD SKETCH<enter>
SKETCH<enter>
```

Use either method to run the routines and answer the menu questions regarding the types of pointing devices, display monitors, plotters, and printers you will be using with the routines.

## 2.6   Configuring the Software

The software must be interfaced with the type of hardware you selected from Chapter 1. This procedure is called *handshaking:* you are introducing the software to the hardware. If you do not have a pointing device, you can use the keyboard arrow keys. The INS key is the pointer button. The PG UP key increases the plotter travel speed by a factor of 5 each time the key is depressed. The PG ON key decreases the travel speed by the same amount. The HOME key moves the pointer to the left end of the menu bar, and the END key returns to the location where HOME was last pressed.
    The pointer is usually connected to a serial port. The plotter shown in Chapter 1 was also connected to a serial port. To avoid confusion during handshaking, assign COM1 to the pointer and COM2 to the plotter. When you configure the plotter, the following screen message appears:

```
Plot connection:
1.  Serial port
2.  Parallel port    or System printer
3.  File
```

Some plotters connect to a serial (RS-232C) communications port at your workstation; others connect to a parallel port. Enter the desired option number and press <enter>. If you elect to use the graphics printer shown in Chapter 1 instead of the plotter, select option 1 (serial). The software will assume that the serial port parameters (bits per second, parity, data bits, stop bits) have been set properly using the DOS MODE command and that it is set for handshaking. Assuming that you have connected to the serial port COM2, the following MODE command establishes the proper port modes for the printers:

```
MODE COM2: 9600,E,7,1<enter>
```

The file option (3) will send material to a disk file for storage so that the sketches can be used later in another chapter.

In this chapter the software stores information about its configuration in a file called SKETCH.CFG. If you want to change the configuration (add or remove a device from the workstation), you can request a configuration dialogue by deleting the SKETCH.CFG file.

## 2.7 Sketching Area

Once the software package has been configured, a sketching area will be displayed as shown in Figure 2.3. At the top of the VDT is a menu bar containing menu names, a

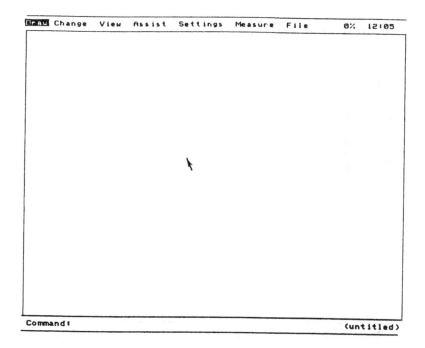

**Figure 2.3** Sketching area and pointer symbol.

memory use meter, and a digital clock. At the bottom is a prompt line. When you use the sketching area, prompt commands are displayed here to remind you what information is expected. The file name of the current sketch is also shown. The sketching area is the area between the menu bar and prompt line.

## 2.8   Using the Pointer

The VDT location of the pointer is displayed as an arrow in Figure 2.3. You will note that the arrow is displayed near the middle of the sketching area. Your pointing device (keyboard, light pen, or mouse) controls the location of the arrow. Try moving it around the VDT. Now move the pointer (arrow) so that it touches the menu bar at DRAW. Notice that DRAW is now highlighted as illustrated in Figure 2.3. When any menu item is highlighted, you may press the selection button on the pointing device to cause a "pull-down" menu to appear. Let's try each of the menu items. As you move from one menu item to another, the last menu pull-down rolls back up.

## 2.9   Selecting a Menu Item

When a menu has been pulled down, as in DRAW, you may move the pointer up and down inside the pull-down to highlight the various items. Pressing the pointer button

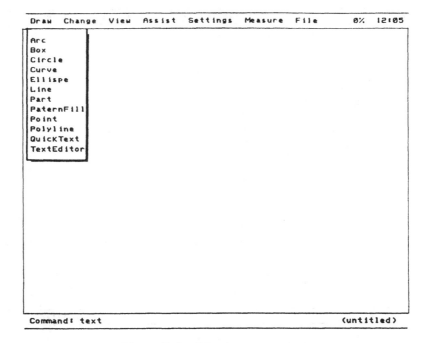

**Figure 2.4**   Selecting a menu item.

while a menu item is highlighted activates that item. Move the pointer down and highlight each of the items shown in Figure 2.4. Notice that as each item is highlighted, it causes the prompt line at the bottom of the VDT to change. For example, at the LINE selection the prompt line read:

```
Line Enter point:
```

In the sections that follow, we try each DRAW menu item as it appears on the pulldown.

## 2.10 ARC Command

An arc is any portion of a circle and is highlighted by the pointer. To display an arc, specify three points inside the sketching area by moving the pointer. Following Figure 2.5, select a start point, a point along the arc, and the arc end point. As you pick the third point, a ghost image of the arc will drag along the VDT as you move the pointer toward the end point. Select the third point and a sharp, permanent arc image appears. The ghost image is called "write-through" graphics and is really considered to be a VDT cursor until a final selection is made. Does your sketching contain three arcs, and

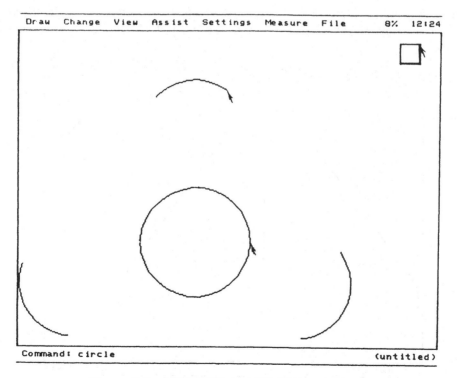

**Figure 2.5** ARC, BOX, and CIRCLE commands.

does it look like Figure 2.5? If it does not, we can move or erase the arc when we come to another pull-down menu item. Leave it for now and continue down the DRAW menu list.

## 2.11  BOX Command

Commonly called a rectangle in other software packages, the BOX command displays rectangular images. You specify the locations of two opposite corners of the box. Following Figure 2.5, place a box around the arc images displayed earlier, making the first box as large as the sketching area. Now place a much smaller box in the upper right-hand corner of the VDT. The box routine is used in other software functions as well. You will use the box concept whenever you place a window on the sketching area.

## 2.12  CIRCLE Command

To display a circle, specify the center point and a point on the edge of the circle. Place the circle image as shown in Figure 2.5. Practice the selection (pick) and location (put) of several CIRCLE commands.

## 2.13  CURVE Command

Commonly called SPLINE or SMOOT in other software packages, the CURVE command accepts several points in succession (a maximum of 100) to define a curved line

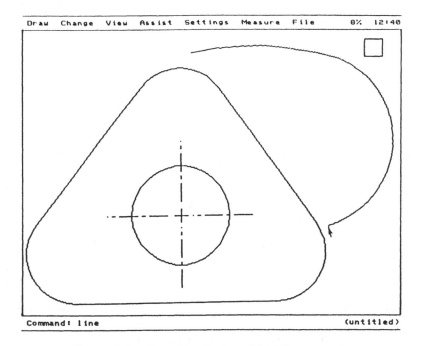

**Figure 2.6**  CURVE, LINE, and PART commands.

image. The points you choose are really control points for the FRAME routine inside the ASSIST menu. FRAME is the logical pattern of point connection: the more points, the smoother the curve displayed. To indicate the end of the points in succession (data stream), choose to identical points or select the first point entered to form a closed spline curve. Follow Figure 2.6 to practice this.

## 2.14   LINE Command

To display a single line, choose the LINE command. The prompt line indicates `Enter point:`. Choose a VDT location and the prompt line reads `To point:`. Pick another location and a line appears between the two points. Notice that as you moved between the two points to choose the second location, a rubber-band-like ghost line followed the pointer arrow. After the second point was selected, a sharp permanent line appeared. Notice also that the prompt line now reads `Enter point:`. This feature was offered before. Whenever you choose an item from the DRAW menu, it stays with that choice until you select another command.

## 2.15   PART Command

The PART menu item allows you to merge a stored sketch into the current sketch. Since this is the first sketch created with this software, we are not able to do this yet. Something called a *dialogue box* will be used from the FILE menu. Later when we practice the FILE menu we will come back to PART commands. For now we need only know that PART is used to create "parts" of sketches, such as symbols or frequently used images, and to reuse them over and over with little effort.

## 2.16   POINT Command

The POINT command places a mark on the VDT where you specify. These VDT locations can be used as node attachment points for library symbols, text locations, or any starting or ending locations. Because they are visible, they are easily located later during sketch construction. Follow Figure 2.7 to display several point locations.

## 2.17   POLYGON Command

Sometimes it is convenient to display polygon shapes of various sizes inside the sketching area. Following Figure 2.8, pick the POLYGON command and place the images as shown. To end the series of lines used to construct the polygon, click the pointer button twice without moving.

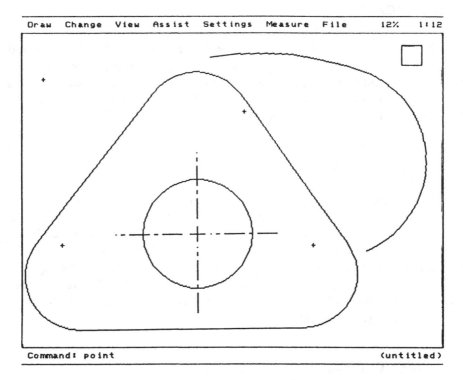

**Figure 2.7** POINT locations.

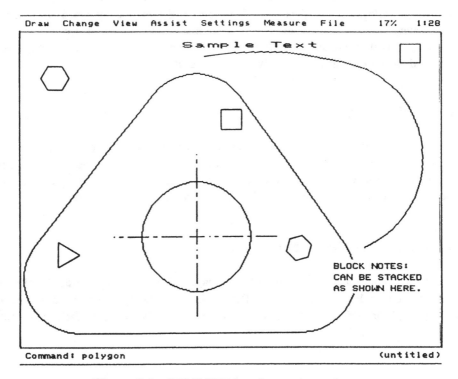

**Figure 2.8** POLYGON locations and sample text.

## 2.18   TEXT Command

Use the TEXT menu item to display the lines of text shown in Figure 2.8. You will notice that the TEXT command appears in two places. Under the SETTINGS menu you may select character height, baseline and obliquing angles, and factors affecting width expansion. When you select this command inside the draw menu, the prompt line asks for text location: this is the left side of the text string. When the location is given, a small line appears on the sketching area at the first character location. As you type the desired text string, the characters appear. If you make a mistake, the backspace key will erase unwanted characters.

Block notes can be created using this command. At the right side of the text, press the control/J keys together and the text line will advance to a new line below the left-side location. In this manner you may type as many lines of notes as needed for the sketch. Follow the example shown in Figure 2.8.

## 2.19   UNDO and REDO Commands

The first command in the CHANGE pull-down menu is the UNDO. This will remove the last drawing menu item. For example, the last drawing item was TEXT; suppose

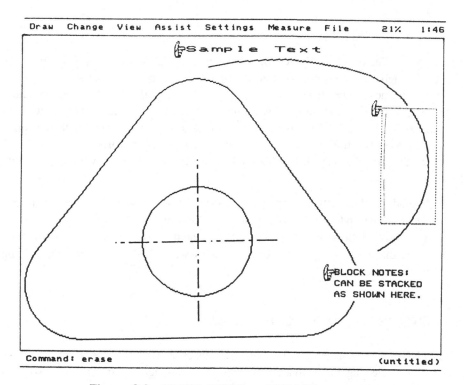

**Figure 2.9**   UNDO, REDO, and ERASE commands.

that we wished to remove that item from the screen. Begin by selecting the CHANGE pull-down menu and placing the pointing arrow over UNDO. Choose that function, so that it is highlighted. Notice in Figure 2.9 that the arrow disappears and a hand pointing to the right appears. The hand pointer signifies that a change is needed. Move the hand pointer so that it touches the `Sample Text` image and press the pointer button.

You can select the change functions in succession to step back through the sketching session just by clicking the pointer button. Because this is so easy, you may remove more than you want, and therefore you may simply reverse the process by selecting the redo function. This of these two commands as off/on or visible/invisible. Practice the use of these two functions.

## 2.20   ERASE Function

Now that we have several draw commands displayed on the screen, let's try erasing a few of them. Select ERASE from the CHANGE menu. Notice that the prompt line reads

    Erase Select objects:

You may begin in the upper portion of the VDT and remove the polygons one at a time by placing the hand pointer on each and pressing the pointer button. Next, move the hand into the open area of the sketching area. Press the pointer butter and the prompt line changes to

    Erase Crosses/window corner:

The point you selected is considered the first corner of a box, and as you move the pointer to the right and upward, you stretch a boxlike window over the sketching area. Stop when you enclose the items you want to erase. You may press the pointer button and the images inside the erase window will disappear. Try that now. If you want to bring them back, choose UNDO and they will return to the screen. Next select an open area. The ERASE function can be used by placing the second corner to the left and upward. Do this now. Notice that a dashed line represents the erase window. The two cases are:

1.   A solid window will erase only those items clearly inside it. If part of an image is inside and part is outside, none of the object is erased.
2.   A dashed window will erase everything that it "crosses" as well as anything inside the window. Try both of these cases with the display objects remaining on the screen.

## 2.21   GROUP and UNGROUP Functions

GROUP/UNGROUP is a change function that makes it easier to operate on a set of objects without selecting the individual objects again and again. For example, suppose

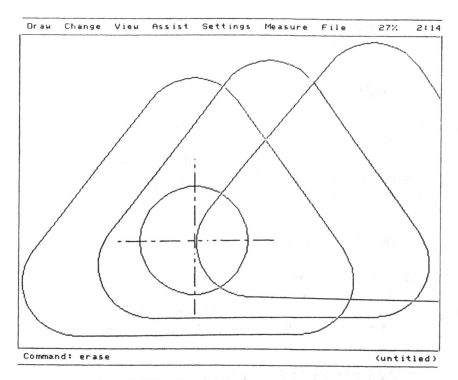

Draw   Change   View   Assist   Settings   Measure   File      27%      2:14

Command: erase                                                    (untitled)

**Figure 2.10**   GROUP, UNGROUP, MOVE, and COPY commands.

that we wanted to use the three arcs and three lines displayed in the lower left-hand corner of the VDT. Begin by selecting the GROUP function, move to an area close to the items to be grouped, press the pointer button, and move the window around the items to be grouped as shown in Figure 2.10. You will notice that they become dotted, to signify that they have become grouped together as a single image. Oncethe group has been selected to be displayed again, they return to the solid-line state.

Grouping may be done at several levels; for example, the items selected as a group may be used together with other VDT images to form a second grouping; and so on. Because this is very useful and powerful in the design sketching stage, it can be overdone; then the groups will need to be broken apart again using the UNGROUP function.

## 2.22   MOVE and COPY Functions

The change functions MOVE and COPY are used to move images or to make as many copies as needed in various locations. You may either point to an object with the hand pointer or put a window around one or more objects. The software package then prompts you for two points and uses the direction and distance from the first point to the second as the new location. Let's practice the use of these functions. Begin by moving the group of objects formed in Figure 2.10. Move the group up and to the right. Then make two copies, each up and to the right.

## 2.23  STRETCH Function

The STRETCH function uses a crosses type of window and requests two points, as in MOVE and COPY. Any objects totally inside the window are moved, and objects crossed are stretched (made longer) as they are moved. Begin this by placing the stretch window around a VDT image. Notice that some of the objects are moved and that others are made longer to fit the distance moved.

## 2.24  PROPERTY Function

The PROPERTY function appears in three different pull-down menus: CHANGE, SETTINGS, and MEASURE. In all three cases a property is either a color, a sketching layer, or a linetype. In Section 2.33 we list the available colors, the choices of sketching layers available, and the linetypes available for use with the sketching software.

## 2.25  ROTATE and SCALE Functions

The ROTATE and SCALE functions allow you to turn existing VDT objects or to shrink or enlarge individual screen objects independently. Begin the process by using the hand pointer to touch the desired object. Next, move the pointer to establish a base point. The software will then ask for a second point and will drag the objects in 1° steps for rotation and steps of .1 for scaling. As you move the pointer along the baseline, you can observe rotation or scaling taking place.

## 2.26  MIRROR Function

Use the MIRROR function to create a mirror image of existing objects in the sketching area. Begin by selecting the image to mirror with the hand pointer. The software will prompt you for the two end points of the mirror line. The object is dragged on the screen as you move the pointer to the end point. The original object remains in place and unchanged.

## 2.27  BREAK Function

One of the most useful sketching techniques is the BREAK function, which allows you to remove portions of display images. You may remove part of a line segment, remove a character from a text string, or provide visibility. To use the BREAK function, point to the VDT objects with the hand pointer. The software will highlight each object and display it using dotted lines. As each object is highlighted, use the pointer to locate two breakpoints on the image. The software removes the portion between the breakpoints. Practice breaking each of the DRAW menu lines.

## 2.28   VIEW Selections

The third pull-down menu at the top of the VDT is the VIEW menu. It contains four basic operational techniques: view, zoom, pan, and redraw. Begin the familiarization process by selecting last view. This operation allows you to jump between the current screen and the screen displayed just prior to the last operation. Because we have not used this pull-down menu earlier in our practice session, it is inactive. After practice with the various zoom, pan, and redraw operations, they can be used successfully.

## 2.29   Zoom Operations

Four types of zoom operations can be used. Begin by selecting the Zoom X operation from the VIEW pull-down menu. Notice that after selection a dialogue box appeared directly in the middle of the display screen. Answer the question about scale factor by entering .5 and pointing at the OK box. Notice that the screen objects have been displayed at one-half size. Select Zoom X again and enter 2.; notice that the objects are now twice their normal size. Select Zoom X a third time and enter 1.; the screen should now appear normal again.

Zoom Box may be selected from the VIEW pull-down menu if only a portion of the display screen needs to be zoomed. After selection you work with a display window as demonstrated for ERASE, GROUP, MOVE, COPY, and STRETCH. Use it the same way. It does not matter whether the second point is to left or the right of the first point. Zoom Limits may be used with the SETTINGS pull-down menu item limits. At this point we have no drawing limits and this operation will be used at the time of demonstration of the SETTINGS menu. Zoom Full fills the screen with the portion of the drawing that currently contains objects.

## 2.30   Pan Operations

Pan may be used to move the entire VDT contents back and forth or up and down. This is very hardy when editing a very large sketch or for moving around inside the sketching area after a Zoom-In has been activated. Remember, Zoom-In is any value greater than 1., and Zoom-Out is any value less than the current Zoom X. Practice the use of Pan.

## 2.31  Redraw Operations

Redraw may be used to clean-up the screen without changing the view. Sketching leaves construction marks, pointer residue, and other break marks on the screen. This selection is the most commonly used software item. Use it now to clean up the viewing area of the figures used thus far in this chapter.

## 2.32  ASSIST Menu

Five sketching tools may be turned on or off during sketching. Begin the process of learning how these work by pulling down the ASSIST menu. If a checkmark appears to the left of any of the five items, that assistance is turned on. To turn an item on or off, move the pointer to it and press the pointer button. You may select these now one at a time and observe the display screen.

1.  *Ortho:* will snap lines directly horizontal and vertical. Select a line from the DRAW menu and practice the use of ortho.
2.  *Frame:* defines the area for a spline. Use it with the curve from the DRAW menu and display some items.

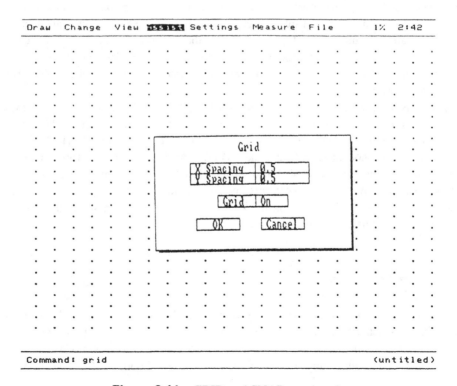

**Figure 2.11**   GRID and SNAP commands.

3. *Grid:* a rectangular grid of dots appears on the screen. Your screen should look like Figure 2.11.

4. *Snap:* works like ortho between the dots. As you move the pointer, a small cross appears to follow it. The cross stops only at a grid location (dot). Therefore, with snap on you can sketch only to the nearest grid location.

5. *Attach:* works like snap for existing objects. When you want to connect a new object, such as a line, to another object, such as a circle, attach selects the closest point possible.

## 2.33   SETTINGS Menu

Several menu items let you change settings and modes by entering values in a dialogue box. A good example of this was Figure 2.11, where we requested a grid background. By changing the values indicated in the various areas of the dialogue box, you can set the spacing for a rectangular grid of dots and turn this grid off and on. As is true for all SETTINGS menu items, the grid contains OK and CANCEL boxes at the bottom. The software waits until you exit teh dialogue box either by selecting the OK box or CANCELing the setting.

SETTINGS menu dialogue boxes have different text messages inside, much as:

1. *Attach:* line, arc, end points, arc midpoints, center and quadrant (0°; 90°; 180°; and 270°) points of circles, and nodes can all be considered attachment points. The dialogue box displayed by this item allows you to toggle each type of attachment point on or off individually. See Section 2.32.

2. *Color:* each screen object can be displayed in a different color. You can select the color name or point to the color number near the bottom of the dialogue box and type in that number. The color numbers are:

   1   Red
   2   Yellow
   3   Green
   4   Cyan
   5   Blue
   6   Magenta
   7   Black

   See Section 2.24.

3. *Curve:* a dialogue box to control precisely how each segment of a spline curve is displayed and provides the on/off control for the frame. The larger the number you enter in the drawing segments box, the smoother the curve that will be displayed. A default value of 8 is presented. See Sections 2.13.

4. *Grid:* see Figure 2.11.

5. *Layer:* a dialogue box for selecting one of 10 layers to be visible or invisible. You can select the current layer, the layer on which anything new is placed. See Section 2.24.

6. *Limits:* permits you to adjust the VDT limits to correspond to the size of sketch that you wish to make. You can set the left, top, and bottom limits. See Section 2.29.

7. *Linetype:* selects the current linetype for sketching new objects. Text and dimensions are always displayed with solid lines, but other objects can be displayed with any of the linetypes available. A linetype is a specific sequence of alternating or continuous line segments or spaces. You select linetypes like colors, to draw attention to important details, highlight changes, or indicate visually the relationships among objects. See Section 2.24.

8. *Part base:* used to set a part (see Section 2.15) reference point before saving the drawing part. The default reference point is (0,0).

9. *Pick:* a dialogue box for setting the hand pointer accuracy.

10. *Property:* see Section 2.24.

11. *Snap:* see Figure 2.11.

12. *Text:* a dialogue box for changing character height, baseline angle, width factor, and obliquing angle. See Section 2.18.

## 2.34  MEASURE Menu

The menu items described next allow you to measure various aspects of a sketch. Some of the items display a result inside a dialogue box: others add dimensions to the sketch. In each MEASURE menu item, the measured value is saved in a system variable for possible use later. The menu items are:

1. *Distance:* two points; stores them as a system variable (/ldist) and calculates the distance between, this value then being displayed in a dialogue box.

2. *Angle:* two points; stores them as a system variable (/angle) and calculates the degrees between, this value then being displayed in a dialogue box.

3. *Area:* series of points; stores the area as (/larea) and displays the result in a dialogue box.

4. *Point:* displays the current coordinates as the pointer is moved on the VDT. When the pointer button is pressed, the location is displayed.

5. *Bearing:* two points; calculates the compass direction and displays the result.

6. *Dimension:* displays an aligned horizontal or vertical dimension between two points. After the two points are centered, a third point indicates the location of the dimension line. Use the last screen display and dimension several of the features in Figure 2.9.

7. *Show properties:* a dialogue box that shows the current object type, layer, color, and linetype.

## 2.35  FILE Menu

The last pull-down menu, FILE, lets you begin a new drawing, load an existing drawing, save or plot the current drawing, create a network drawing interchange file, or quit.

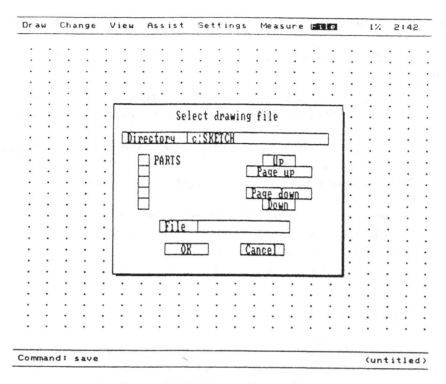

Draw　Change　View　Assist　Settings　Measure　File　　1%　2:42

Command: save　　　　　　　　　　　　　　　　　　　　(untitled)

**Figure 2.12**　Film menu dialogue box.

We begin exploring this pull-down by selecting the new command. This will terminate the series of example figures that we have created so far in this chapter. A dialogue box will appear as soon as we select NEW because there is information currently on the screen. You can now save the last sketch, as shown in Figure 2.10, by selecting the SAVE command from the pull-down menu. Since we have not given our series of figures a name (untitled), a SAVEAS dialogue box appears. Point to the file name box and type in a drawing name. The name can be no longer than eight characters and may contain letters, digits, and the special symbols $, -, and _. For example, FIRSTONE is a perfect name for this first sketch. Point to the OK box, and the sketch is saved.

The OPEN command retrieves a saved drawing to view or edit. Let's clear the screen for a new sketch and try retrieving the sketch that we just saved. Pick NEW from the menu; we just saved it, so NEW won't complain. We now have a fresh screen. To retrieve the saved drawing, select OPEN: this displays the dialogue box shown in Figure 2.12. At the top is the directory box; near the bottom is the file name box, with nothing in it. Point to th file box and type FIRSTONE. Now select the OK box at the bottom of the dialogue box and the sketch called FIRSTONE is displayed on the VDT.

## 2.36   Other File Functions

Depending on the configuration of the software in Section 2.6, you will be able to do the following:

1. *Make DXF:* a file function selected to make a drawing interchange format files using the current sketch. These files can then be used in any of the remaining chapters.
2. *Pen info:* a dialogue box for selecting pen numbers to be used with the plotter described in Chapter 1.
3. *Plot area:* a dialogue box for selecting paper size, measurement units, and scale factor for the plotter.
4. *Plot name:* lets you set the plot-out name for this sketch.
5. *Information:* displays the number of the current version (3.0).
6. *Game:* dialogue box containing chapter exercises.
7. *Quit:* returns to the operating system.

## 2.37   Memory Use Meter

The software keeps the entire sketch in memory, so the complexity of a sketch is limited by the amount of memory in your workstation. Toward the right end of the menu bar is the memory use meter. In Figure 2.4 it read 0%. As you sketch objects, making the screen more complex, this percentage will grow.

## 2.38   Digital Clock

The last item on the menu bar is the digital clock. The time will be correct only if your computer's clock has been set properly.

## Exercises

Try to simulate each of the following display screens.

1. _____        2.

3.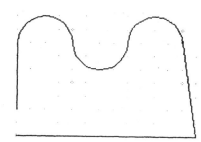

4.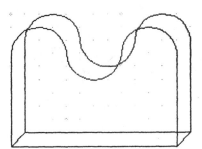

5.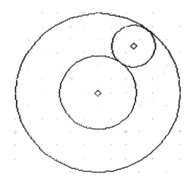

6.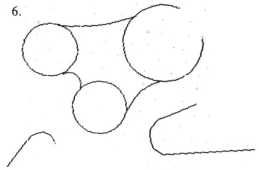

7.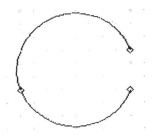

8.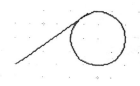

9.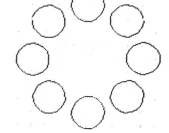

10.

11.

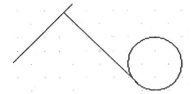

12.

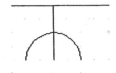

13.

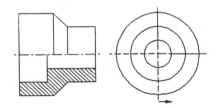

14.

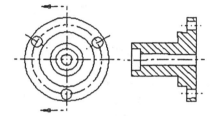

15.

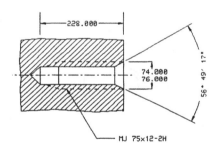

16.

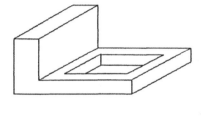

17.

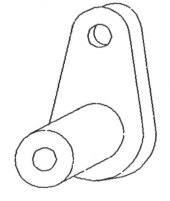

18.

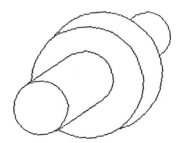

19.

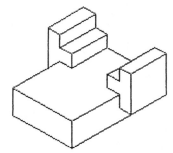

20.

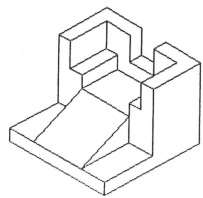

# 3

# Computerizing the Design Process

To computerize the industrial design process, the design language structure for a computer-aided design display has to be a series of commands that move the VDT beam, plotter pen, or tool path such that the end result is a properly drawn design, working drawing, or finished production part. In Chapter 2 we concentrated on the design sketch and how to produce it. In this chapter we focus on the finished production part. The remainder of the book covers the concepts basic to computer-aided design (CAD). The concepts in this chapter are basic to computer-aided engineering (CAE) and are illustrated in Figure 3.1. A design prepares the design layout so that the computer can automatically generate parts lists, detail drawings, location and clearance fit checks, and assembly drawings. CAE is not an end in itself; handled properly, it is the beginning of a sequence that includes graphics, design, and production or manufacture. The basis of CAE is to communicate design intent. If the engineer is unaware of the method diagrammed in Figure 3.1, CAE is not possible. The CAE technique allows us to include all the information for design analysis (testing), prototype construction (experimentation), and manufacture of a product.

## 3.1  CAE Software Network

If we assume that the software used in the first two chapters is only one part of a total software network, CADD is only one of several functions of that network. Manufactur-

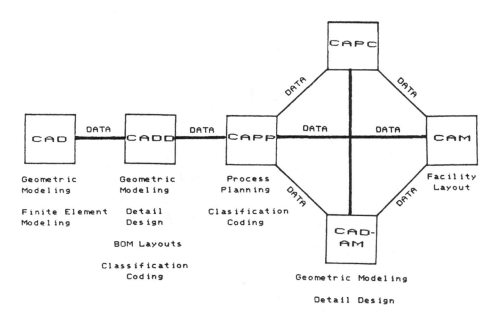

**Figure 3.1**  CAE design and manufacturing network.

ing planning (CAPP), production control (CPAC), tool design (CADAM), and manufacturing operations (CAM) follow CADD and CAE. Note in Figure 3.1 that a stream of information connects all these functions: it is the database for the entire network. Although this book is particular in its treatment of the CADD and CAD functions, the other functions cannot be ignored. All CADD personnel must understand how the network is organized so that they can get information from and put information into the database. Figure 3.2 is a good illustration of the total database network. Notice that it is divided into 2D, 3D, and nongraphic. When Figures 3.1 and 3.2 are compared, an understanding of the function is clear. In Figure 3.1, starting at the left of the diagram, CAD has two primary data types:

1. Geometric (input)
2. Finite element (input–output)

Moving to the right, CADD has five primary data types:

1. Geometric (shared with CAD, input for all drawings)
2. Detail design (output)
3. Bill of materials (input to CADD)
4. Layout drawings (input to CAPC and CAM)
5. Classification coding (input to CADAM and CAM)

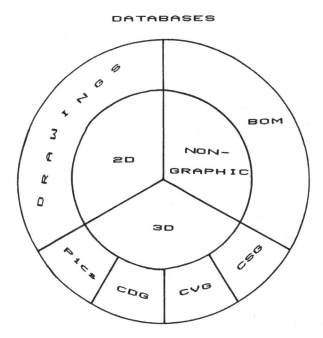

**Figure 3.2** Database components.

Moving along the network, computer-aided process planning (CAPP) has two primary data types:

1. Process planning (input, CADD; output, CAPP and CADAM)
2. Classification coding

The network branches into production control (CAPP), tool design (CADAM), and manufacturing operations (CAM), which have four primary data types:

1. Geometric (input, CAD and CADD)
2. Detail design
3. CADAM
4. CAM

## 3.2 Database Components

Figure 3.2 gives us a good representation of the types of databases and how they are used. In this book the representation is:

1. *2D*: engineering drawings of all types (Chapters 4, 9, and 10)
2. *3D*: pictorials (Chapter 5), CDG (Chapter 6), CVG (Chapter 7), and CSG (Chapter 8)

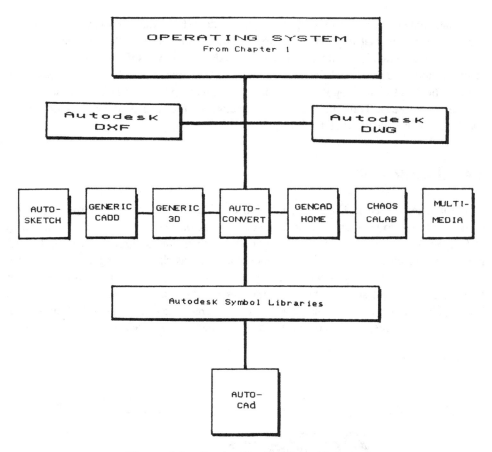

**Figure 3.3** Textbook software architecture.

3. *Nongraphic*: bills of materials and schedules of all types

These data components are used within a wide range of Autodesk-compatible software, as diagrammed in Figure 3.3.

## 3.3 Textbook Software

The software used in this book is outlined in Figure 3.3. Any operating system listed in Chapter 1 can be used on the workstation as the various pieces of software are installed. Two primary types of software files are established, DXF and DWG. These types are translated by AutoConvert, a seamless link to the Autodesk symbol libraries and AutoCAD as well as to the other software listings in Figure 3.3. For AutoSketch (SKD files created in Chapter 2), it is the answer to improving or exporting your drawings to AutoCAD.

AutoConvert comes with support for the Autodesk products shown in Figure 3.3 and other software that imports or exports in DXF, including CADD packages, illustration programs, scanning software, and even CAM and CAE software purchased from other vendors. You will find the user interface easy to follow, thanks to its menu-driven file selection and mouse support. Most of all, you will find the program flexible enough to meet your needs. Translating an entire directory of files can be done by setting it up and letting it run unattended for hours.

## 3.4 Generic CADD

Like AutoSketch used in Chapter 2, the Generic CADD software takes surprisingly little money and time to get started. It is designed to work on the graphics workstation shown in Chapter 1, so you will not need to upgrade your existing equipment. Generic CADD gives a higher-quality finished look to your drawings, as shown in Figure 3.4. When it comes to time savings, you will find this easy to install; follow the outline used for Chapter 2. You will spend only a few minutes installing the software, then jump right into creating your drawings. Thanks to its logical screen interface (shown in Figure 3.4), on-line help features, and a complete, hands-on tutorial, this package is comfortable to use.

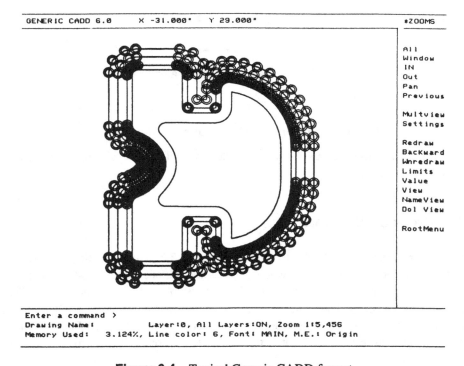

**Figure 3.4** Typical Generic CADD format.

One of its biggest selling points is its set of sophisticated drawing and editing tools. It contains the kind of powerful features normally found in only the most expensive CADD packages, such as AutoCAD. It also comes with nested commands, 256 layers to work on, named layers, multiple viewports, hatch patterns, associative dimensioning, versatile text handling, and strong support for symbols and symbol attributes. You also get a powerful bill of materials (BOM) generation utility for extracting information from your drawing quickly and producing equipment schedules as shown in Figure 3.2.

## 3.5  Generic 3D

The Generic 3D package is a conceptual design tool that lets you create three-dimensional models as called for in Figure 3.1. Designed to be used with Generic CADD 6.0, you can design and nagivate yourself anywhere in your model and in space. Uses for this product range from that of a main presentation tool for new manufactured products to inspection of design intent. You can create isometric or perspective views from virtually any angle, as shown in Figure 3.5.

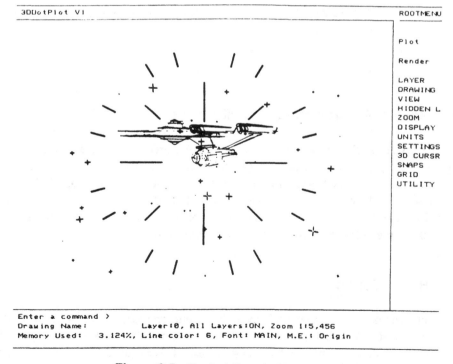

**Figure 3.5**  Typical Generic 3D format.

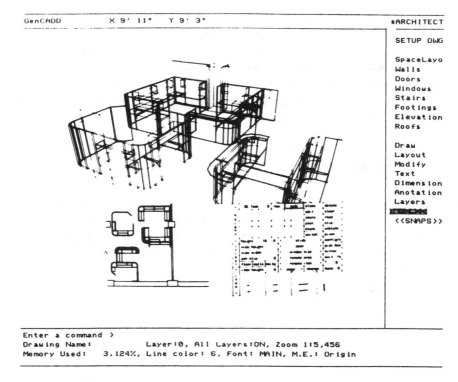

GenCADD          X 9' 11"    Y 9' 3"                                    #ARCHITECT

SETUP DWG

SpaceLayo
Walls
Doors
Windows
Stairs
Footings
Elevation
Roofs

Draw
Layout
Modify
Text
Dimension
Anotation
Layers

<<SNAPS>>

Enter a command >
Drawing Name:              Layer:0, All Layers:ON, Zoom 1:5,456
Memory Used:      3.124%, Line color: 6, Font: MAIN, M.E.: Origin

**Figure 3.6**   Typical GenCADD architectural format.

## 3.6   GenCADD Architectural/Civil Series

The GenCADD Architectural/Civil series is used by architects, space planners, home builders, facility planners, interior designers, landscape architects, and civil engineers. From fieldbook to finished drawings, the COGO option generates site maps and finished detail drawings. Floor plans, elevations, door and window schedules, automatic stair generation, and roof lines are only a small portion of the work done in this package. The package presentation format is shown in Figure 3.6.

## 3.7   Home Series

The Home series contains Home, Kitchen, Bathroom, and Landscape. As illustrated in Figure 3.7, you can design your yard with this package. This package is intended for the home computer user, not for the industrial user. It is included here only to indicate the complete line of software available through a single vender.

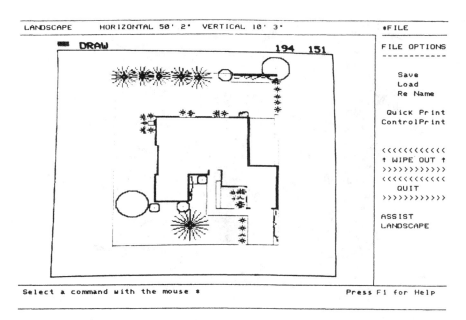

**Figure 3.7** Typical Home series format.

## 3.8 Chaos/CA Lab

Chaos and the CA Lab allow you to present James Gleick's cellular automata based on mathematical progression. This allows you to begin with an initial pattern, then update it repeatedly according to the mathematical expression, rule, or parameter, as shown in Figure 3.8. Scientists use this approach to study cancer cells, growth patterns, and cell structures. It is useful in manufacturing research and material treatment during heat treatment, foundry operations, and the like.

## 3.9 Multimedia Explorer

With Multimedia Explorer you can make high-quality business presentations. The charts and graphs shown throughout Chapter 9 can be reviewed and studied for examples of the use of this software. This package and the others described above share the Autodesk symbol library and the power of a large expensive CAD package, AutoCAD. A few of the symbol types are shown in Figure 3.9. In the remainder of the book we describe use of the AutoCAD package.

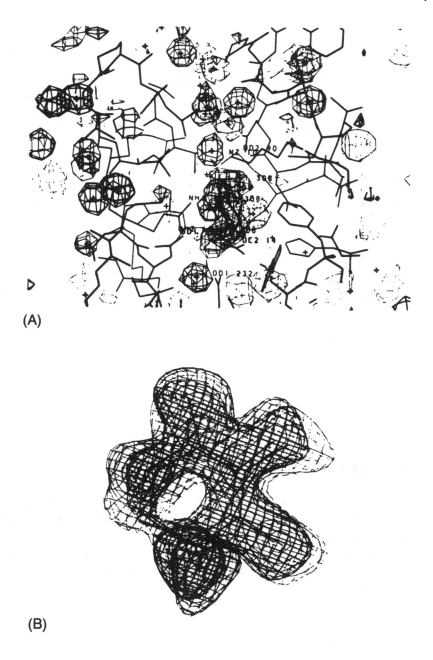

(A)

(B)

**Figure 3.8**   Example outputs from Chaos and CA Lab.

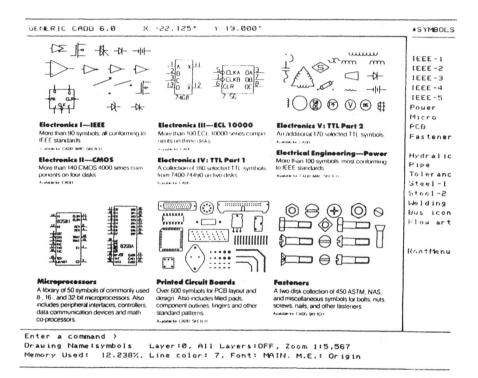

**Figure 3.9** Sample symbols ouput.

## 3.10   Manufacturing Operations

A computer-aided design and manufacturing operation requires that certain concepts be displayed at the VDT of the graphics terminal. The manufacturing tasks presented here are:

| Task | Function | Figure |
|------|----------|--------|
| ANGLE | Modification of rotation | 3.10 |
| ARC | Tool moving about radius | 3.11 |
| ATANGLE | Display other than THETA | 3.12 |
| BEARG | Bearing tool displacement | 3.13 |
| CENTER | Indicates tool travel | 3.14 |
| CYLIND | Circular cylinder tool form | 3.15 |
| DATAPT | Space location in 3D | 3.16 |
| DOT | Tool point—solid object | 3.18 |
| GOTO | Tool control | 3.19 |
| HOME | Origin of tool position | 3.20 |
| IN | Inside tolerance for tool | 3.21 |
| LINES | Tool path displacement | 3.23 |
| OUT | Outside tolerance for tool | 3.22 |
| PLANE | Three or more DATAPTS | 3.24 |
| PT | 2D space location | 3.17 |
| R | Radius of part feature | 3.25 |
| RTHETA | Arc segments along radius | 3.26 |
| SLOPE | Angle in degrees of feature | 3.27 |
| TANTO | Tangent to | 3.28 |
| UNIT | Display element size | 3.29 |
| VECTOR | Part properties | 3.30 |
| XYZPLAN | Surfaces on a planning model | 3.31 |

## 3.11   ANGLE

The CADAM function ANGLE is used to describe any angle less than 90° that is measured from the intersection of two axes on a 2D plane within a 3D model. See Figure 3.10.

## 3.12   ARC

The ARC function generates a tool path that is composed of tangential slope lines to the desired or true arc. As indicated in Chapter 2, these lines cover minute distances that change rapidly for tool control. See Figure 3.11.

## 3.13   ATANGLE

All angles greater than 90° are displayed as shown in Figure 3.12.

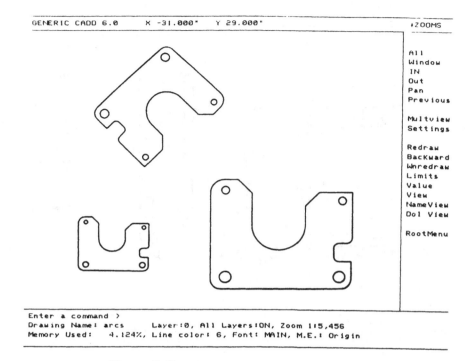

**Figure 3.10**  Typical use of ANGLE methods.

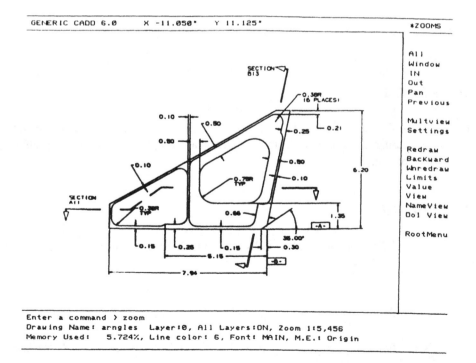

**Figure 3.11**  Typical use of ARC commands.

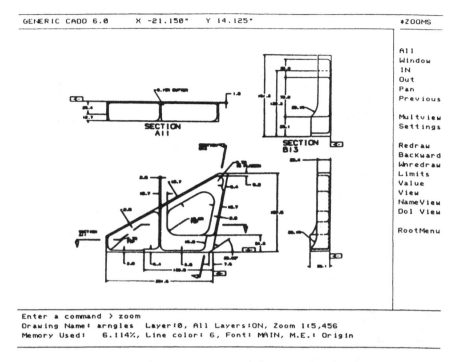

**Figure 3.12**   Continued use of ATANGLE methods.

## 3.14   BEARG

The piece part shown in Figure 3.13 is typical of the use for the CADAM function BEARG. A bearing angle is read from the horizontal viewport and helps in specifications for the tooling.

## 3.15   CENTER

The centerline of the tool path is always displayed in whatever geometry pattern the tool takes, as in Figure 3.14.

## 3.16   CYLIND

Several display functions are shown in Figure 3.15. Study them for use with the exercises at the end of the chapter.

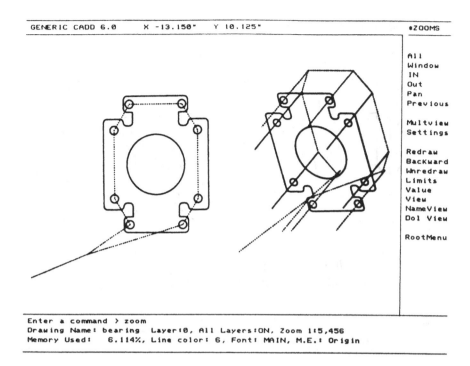

GENERIC CADD 6.0     X -13.150"    Y 10.125"                    *ZOOMS

All
Window
IN
Out
Pan
Previous

Multview
Settings

Redraw
Backward
Whredraw
Limits
Value
View
NameView
Dol View

RootMenu

Enter a command > zoom
Drawing Name: bearing   Layer:0, All Layers:ON, Zoom 1:5,456
Memory Used:   6.114%, Line color: 6, Font: MAIN, M.E.: Origin

**Figure 3.13**   Bearing of a line or start point.

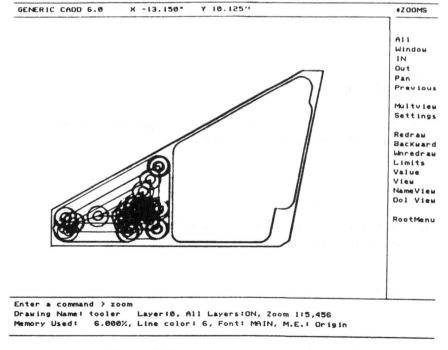

GENERIC CADD 6.0     X -13.150"    Y 10.125"                    *ZOOMS

All
Window
IN
Out
Pan
Previous

Multview
Settings

Redraw
Backward
Whredraw
Limits
Value
View
NameView
Dol View

RootMenu

Enter a command > zoom
Drawing Name: tooler   Layer:0, All Layers:ON, Zoom 1:5,456
Memory Used:   6.000%, Line color: 6, Font: MAIN, M.E.: Origin

**Figure 3.14**   Tool travel: use of CENTER.

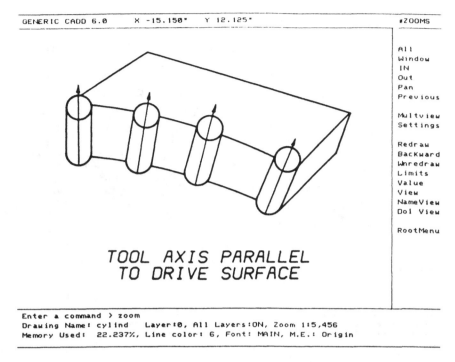

GENERIC CADD 6.0    X -15.150"   Y 12.125"                    #ZOOMS

*TOOL AXIS PARALLEL*
*TO DRIVE SURFACE*

Enter a command > zoom
Drawing Name: cylind    Layer:0, All Layers:ON, Zoom 1:5,456
Memory Used:  22.237%, Line color: 6, Font: MAIN, M.E.: Origin

**Figure 3.15**   Tool form: use of CYLIND.

## 3.17  DATAPT and PT

A data point is a 3D location for a point, expressed in display units and direction of tool travel. See Figure 3.16 for 3D, Figure 3.17 for 2D.

## 3.18  DOT

The current location of a tool point location can be shown as the intersection of a plane and a cylinder, as in Figure 3.18.

## 3.19  GOTO

GOTO is a command issued to move the tool on the face of the VDT at the graphics workstation. See Figure 3.19.

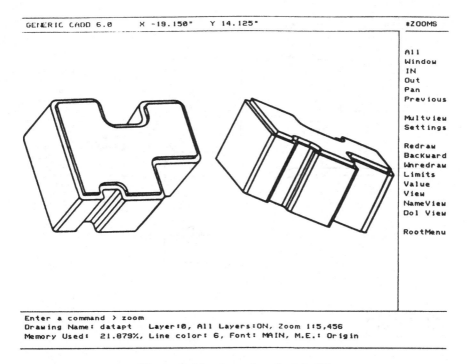

**Figure 3.16** Space locations in 3D.

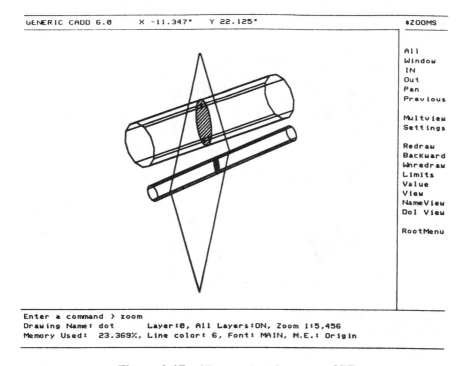

**Figure 3.17** 2D space locations: use of PT.

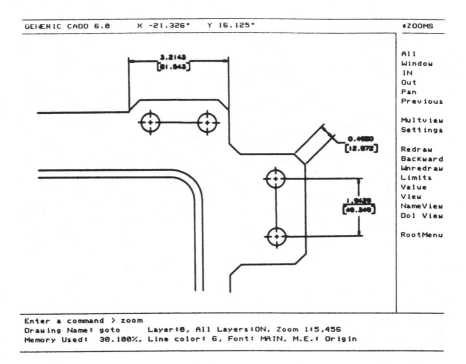

**Figure 3.18**  Tool point—solid object.

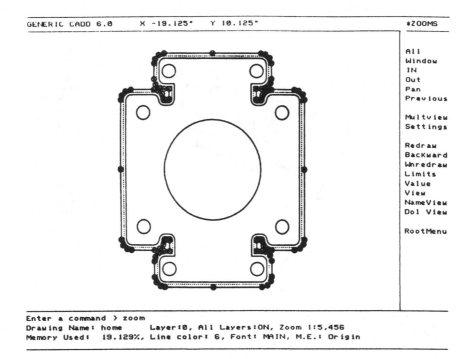

**Figure 3.19**  Tool control: use of GOTO.

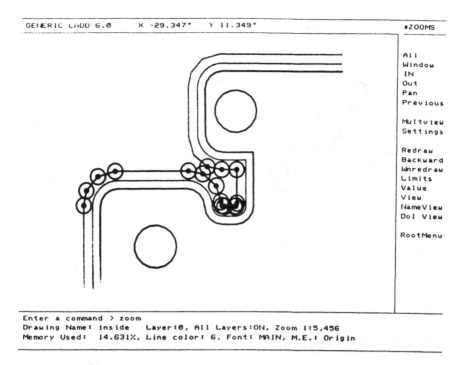

**Figure 3.20**  Origin for tool position: use of HOME.

## 3.20  HOME

The command GO HOME will send the tool just displayed to its starting location. See Figure 3.20.

## 3.21  IN and OUT

Figure 3.21 illustrates the innermost tolerance zone for tool locations during machine processing. Figure 3.22 is the outside of the zone.

## 3.22  LINES

Figure 3.23 gives the tool path total displacement.

## 3.23  PLANE

Figure 3.24 is a display of the plane surface of a part feature.

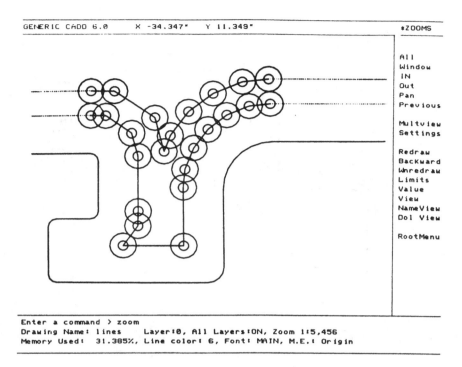

**Figure 3.21**   Inside tolerance for tool: use of IN.

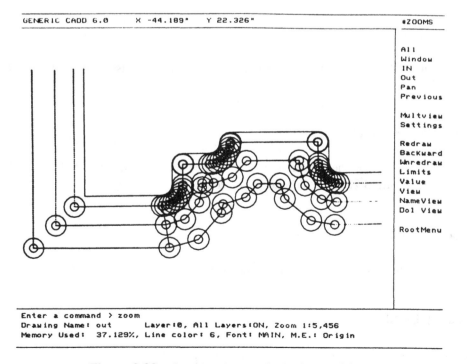

**Figure 3.22**   Outside tolerance for tool: use of OUT.

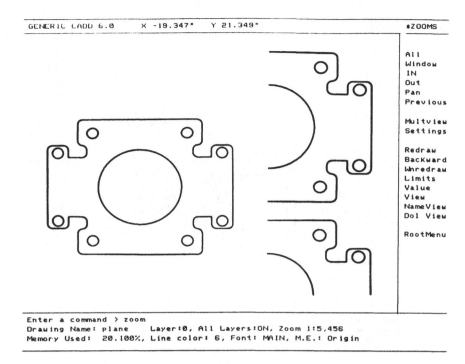

**Figure 3.23** Tool path displacement: use of LINES.

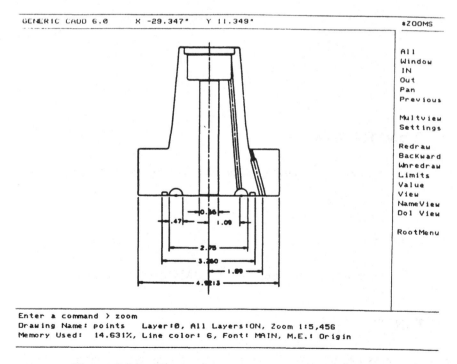

**Figure 3.24** Example of plane surfaces: use of PLANE.

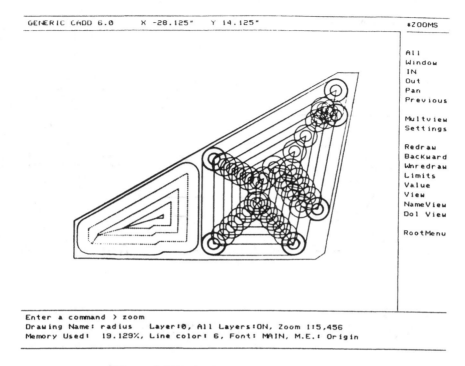

GENERIC CADD 6.0     X -28.125"   Y 14.125"                    *ZOOMS

Enter a command > zoom
Drawing Name: radius    Layer:0, All Layers:ON, Zoom 1:5,456
Memory Used: 19.129%, Line color: 6, Font: MAIN, M.E.: Origin

**Figure 3.25**   Radius of part feature: use of R.

## 3.24   R and RTHETA

Figure 3.25 illustrates the CADAM function R, and Figure 3.26 shows the use of RTHETA.

## 3.25   SLOPE

Figure 3.27 is an example of the use of the CADAM function SLOPE.

## 3.26   TANTO

Figure 3.28 shows two objects (part features) that contain tangent plane surfaces.

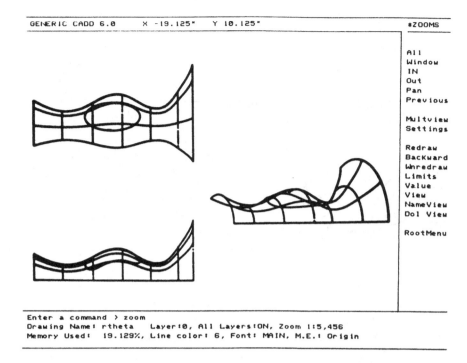

GENERIC CADD 6.0     X -19.125"    Y 10.125"                              #ZOOMS

All
Window
IN
Out
Pan
Previous

Multview
Settings

Redraw
Backward
Unredraw
Limits
Value
View
NameView
Del View

RootMenu

Enter a command > zoom
Drawing Name: rtheta    Layer:0, All Layers:ON, Zoom 1:5,456
Memory Used:  19.129%, Line color: 6, Font: MAIN, M.E.: Origin

**Figure 3.26** Arc segments along a radius: use of RTHETA.

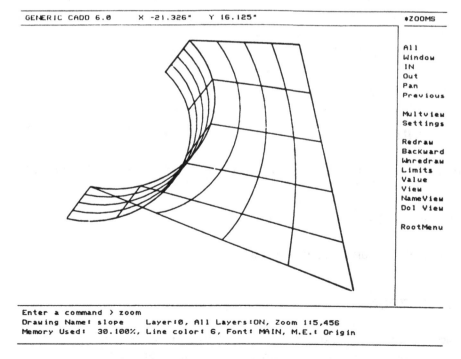

GENERIC CADD 6.0     X -21.326"    Y 16.125"                              #ZOOMS

All
Window
IN
Out
Pan
Previous

Multview
Settings

Redraw
Backward
Unredraw
Limits
Value
View
NameView
Del View

RootMenu

Enter a command > zoom
Drawing Name: slope     Layer:0, All Layers:ON, Zoom 1:5,456
Memory Used:  30.100%, Line color: 6, Font: MAIN, M.E.: Origin

**Figure 3.27** SLOPE to find angle of part feature.

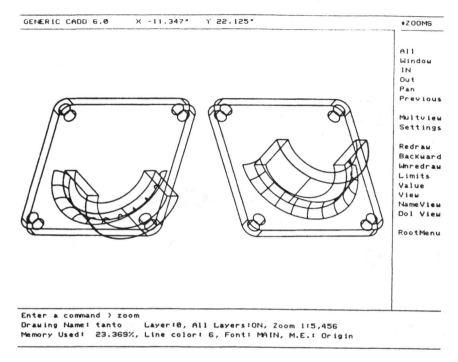

GENERIC CADD 6.0      X -11.347"    Y 22.125"                      *ZOOMS

```
Enter a command > zoom
Drawing Name: tanto     Layer:0, All Layers:ON, Zoom 1:5,456
Memory Used:  23.369%, Line color: 6, Font: MAIN, M.E.: Origin
```

**Figure 3.28**   Plane tangent to a plane: use of TANTO.

## 3.27   UNIT

Part feature are sized by the UNIT function and are demonstrated in Figure 3.29.

## 3.28   VECTOR

Part properties are displayed as shown in Figure 3.30.

## 3.29   XYZPLAN

Surfaces on a planning, geometric, or solid model do not have to be parallel to the X, Y, or Z surfaces. They can be displayed as shown in Figure 3.31.

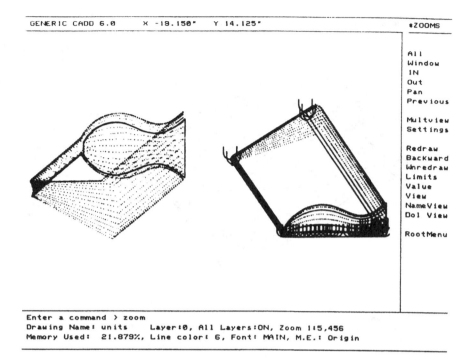

**Figure 3.29**  Display element size: use of UNIT.

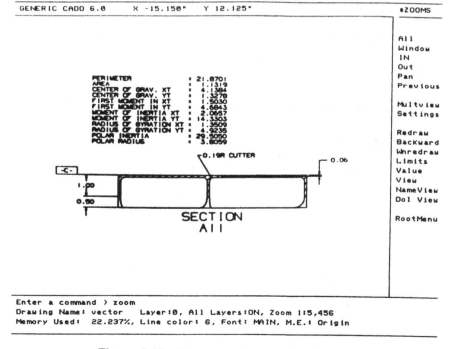

**Figure 3.30**  Part properties: use of VECTOR.

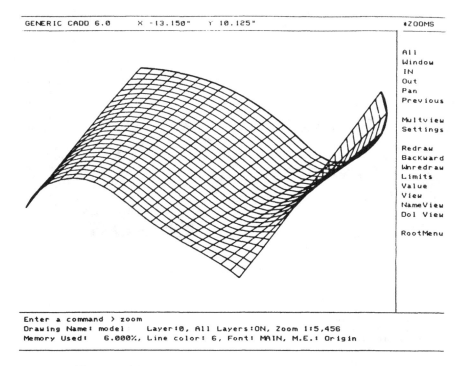

**Figure 3.31**  XYZPLAN example of surfaces on a model.

## Exercises

Try to simulate each of the following display screens.

1.  Basic design entities

2. Offset spline

3. Offset surface

4. Mechanical design

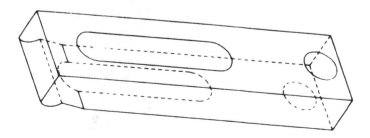

5.   Parts explosion

6.   Hatch design

7.   Surface to surface intersection

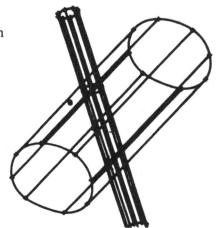

8. Plane projection

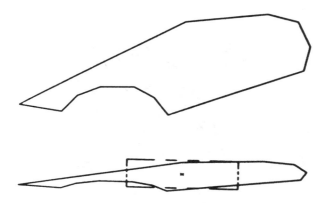

9. Facilities layout

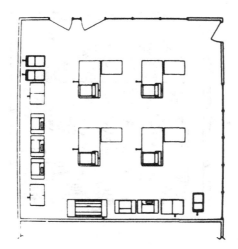

10. Equipment arrangement

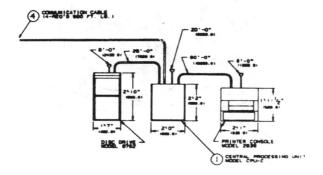

11. Plane mesh intersection

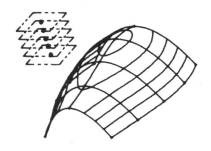

12. Plate mold

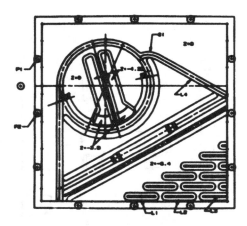

13. Rib milling

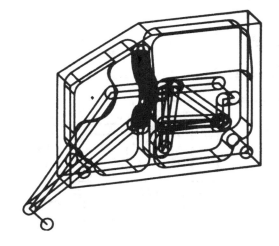

14. Fuel support bracket, end view

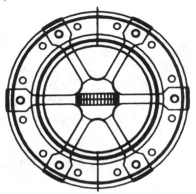

15. Fuel support bracket assembly

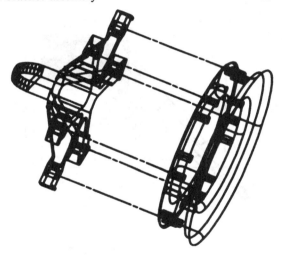

16. Transform duplicates

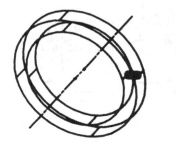 

17.  Fuel mixer

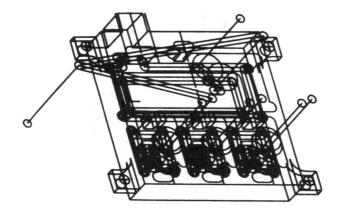

18.  Slant floor kellering

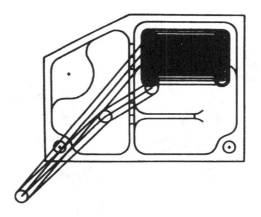

19.  Pocket floor roughing

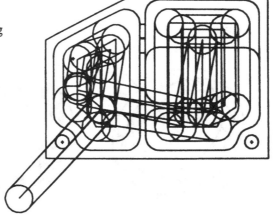

20.   Profile milling

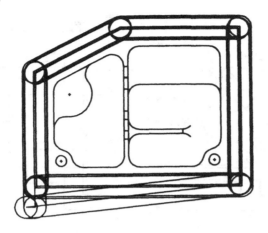

21.   Future check

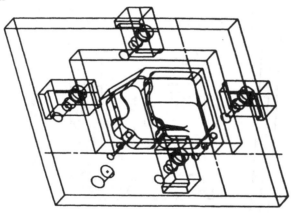

22.   Mechanical detail

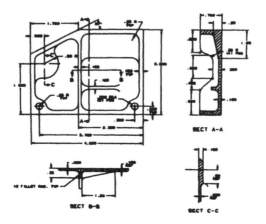

23.    Detail drafting

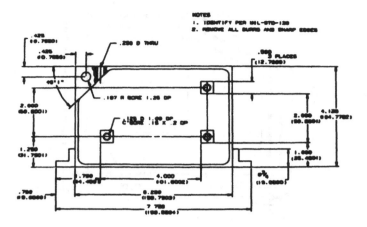

24.    Site plan

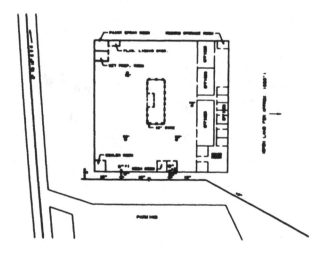

# 4

# Graphics Systems and Software

In this chapter we complete our description of the software architecture that we introduced in Chapter 3. AutoCAD is the largest single and most expensive software package available from Autodesk. The AutoCAD package is only one of several available; see Chapter 3 for the entire list of packages and their relationships. If a package other than AutoCAD is used, it is recommended that the operational manual for that software be used in place of this chapter.

For those who complete the first four chapters of this book based on Autodesk software, the following list of topics will seem natural:

1. Workstation/loading CADD packages with operating system
2. Menu operation and graphics editors
3. Command and/or data entries
4. Coordinate systems and pointing
5. Utility and shell commands
6. Entity commands to create diagrams
7. Inquiry commands for design modifications
8. Display controls for diagram manipulation
9. Layers, colors, and linetypes
10. Drawing aids: grid, snap, ortho, and others

11.  Complex objects and library symbols
12.  Design features: annotation, dimensions, and shading

## 4.1  Using the Menus

You already know how to use side menus, command lines, and pull-down menu items as well as the steps involving copyright laws, installation procedures, and the like. You can refer back to our discussion of any of these, if necessary. In this chapter we study additional software items used in a graphics system to create the following:

1.  Detail drawings with multiviews
2.  Sectional views
3.  Dimensioning and notation
4.  Threads and fasteners

Begin your drawing session in front of the workstation and follow the installation instructions for AutoCAD. When you have finished the configuration file and entered AutoCAD from the main menu, your VDT should look as shown in Figure 4.1. The top of the VDT screen contains

```
Layer 0       0.0000,0.0000
```

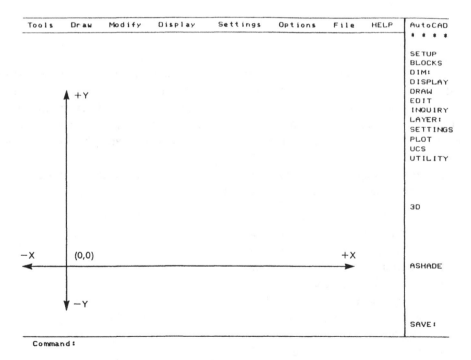

**Figure 4.1**   Graphics screen with cursor located at 0.000,0.000.

where the current drawing layer is zero and the current cursor location is 0.0 in X and 0.0 in Y. Called the *status line,* this can be changed to read

| Tools | Draw | Modify | Display | Settings | Options | File | HELP |
|-------|------|--------|---------|----------|---------|------|------|

by moving the screen cursor over the status line and clicking the mouse pick button. The pull-down menus will now stay in place until you turn them off. You may want to go through each of these pull-down items now to see how they compare with those in AutoSketch discussed in Chapter 2. You will notice first a number of additional commands with which you are not familiar. Table 4.1 is a listing of both AutoSketch and AutoCAD commands, with those in common marked for your reference. You need study only those unique to this chapter.

Autodesk provides an additional method of menu selection when you purchase the software. Called the *tablet menu,* it is shown in Figure 4.2. If your workstation contains a graphics tablet, you may stop and place this menu on the surface of that tablet. You now have a third location where menu items may be selected <pull-down, side of VDT, and tablet>. Drafting and design users generally select one of the three location options for entering commands. Commands are rarely typed from the keyboard because of the time lost in selecting drafting functions.

We do not need to give examples of how to use all four methods of command selection; you may assume that commands are entered in whatever manner is available and suitable for you. Before we progress into the applications for this software and the remainder of this chapter, let's go through the list of items shown on the side menu in

**Table 4.1**  AutoSketch and AutoCAD Commands

HELP Listing

```
        Command List   (+n = ADE-n feature, ' = transparent command)

    APERTURE +2   DELAY         FILLET +1    MENU        * REDO       * STRETCH +3
  * ARC           DIM/DIM1 +1   'GRAPHSCR    MINSERT     * 'REDRAW     STYLE
    AREA          DIST        * GRID       * MIRROR +2    REGEN        TABLET
    ARRAY         DIVIDE +3     HATCH +1   * MOVE         REGENAUTO   *TEXT
    ATTDEF +2     DONUT +3    *'HELP / '?   MSLIDE +2     RENAME      'TEXTSCR
    ATTDISP +2    DOUGHNUT +3   HIDE +3      OFFSET +3    'RESUME      TIME
    ATTEDIT +2    DRAGMODE +2   ID           OOPS       * ROTATE +3    TRACE
    ATTEXT +2     DTEXT +3      IGESIN +3  * ORTHO        RSCRIPT      TRIM +3
    AXIS +1       DXBIN +3      IGESOUT +3   OSNAP +2   * SAVE         U
    BASE          DXFIN         INSERT     * 'PAN       * SCALE +3    *UNDO
    BLIPMODE      DXFOUT        ISOPLANE +2  PEDIT +3     SCRIPT       UNITS +1
    BLOCK         ELEV +3     * LAYER        PLINE +3     SELECT     * 'VIEW +2
  * BREAK +1      ELLIPSE +3  * LIMITS     * PLOT        'SETVAR       VIEWRES
    CHAMFER +1    END         * LINE       * POINT        SHAPE        VPOINT +3
    CHANGE      * ERASE      * LINETYPE   * POLYGON +3    SHELL/SH +3  VSLIDE
  * CIRCLE        EXPLODE +3    LIST         PRPLOT       SKETCH +1    WBLOCK
  * COLOR         EXTEND +3     LOAD         PURGE      * SNAP        * 'ZOOM
  * COPY          FILES         LTSCALE      QTEXT        SOLID        3DFACE
    DBLIST        FILL          MEASURE +3   QUIT         STATUS       3DLINE

At the "Command:" prompt, you can enter RETURN to repeat the last command.

Press RETURN for further help.

* common to AutoSketch
```

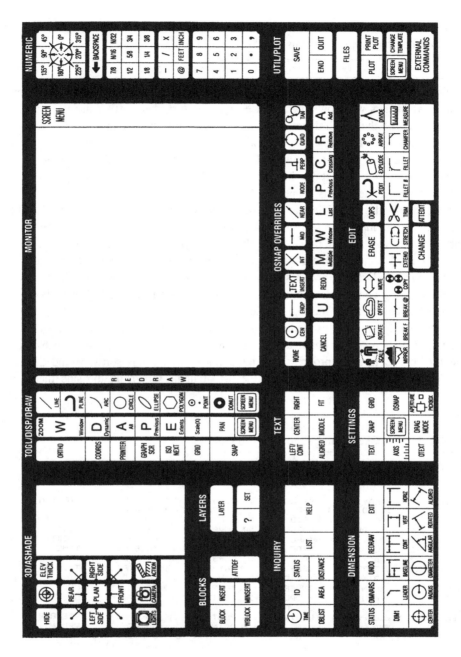

**Figure 4.2** Tablet menu provided by Autodesk with software purchase.

Figure 4.1. With this review you will learn how AutoCAD software functions. We begin with the first item listed in the side menu: AutoCAD. When the screen cursor is placed over this item and pressed, the side, root menu can always be recalled. Try this now. So if all else fails when preparing drawings, always remember that AutoCAD will return you to the main menu. The second item * * * *, can be used to select one or more object snap modes. Try this now. The root menu has been replaced by the items listed in Figure 4.3. Notice that AutoCAD and * * * * stayed in place.

After you have selected items from the * * * * submenu, the previous menu page will reappear automatically with _LAST_, in this case the root menu. If the root menu does not reappear, select AutoCAD.

## 4.2 SETUP Menu Item

The root menu contains a SETUP item (third listed) for defining the scale and boundaries of your drawing. Using this item, you can select a final paper size and scale for plotting/printing your drawing, using architectural, engineering, or metric (decimal) no-

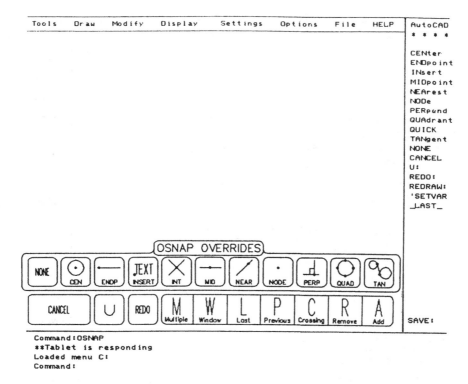

**Figure 4.3** Testing * * * * and tablet menu from Figure 2.

tation as shown in Figure 4.4. You may also set drawing limits and snap spacing to appropriate values, and specify the type of border inside a file called BORDER.DWG. This must be saved prior to selecting SETUP from the root menu. .DGW creation was covered in Chapter 3 and may have to be reviewed before processing further.

## 4.3  BLOCKS Menu Item

Point to BLOCKS in the root menu and press. The menu changes as shown in Figure 4.5. You may have noticed something at this point: if a menu item ends with a :, it has a submenu. Notice that each of the items listed in the BLOCKS root menu has a submenu. These are used in later chapters. Let's begin by selecting ATTDEF, which stands for "attribute definition." Notice in the command/prompt area that attributes have three optional modes, described as follows:

1.  INVISIBLE. This mode is useful if you are not interested in seeing the text listing the attributes of the blocks being displayed on the screen. A block is directly comparable with a group from Chapter 2.

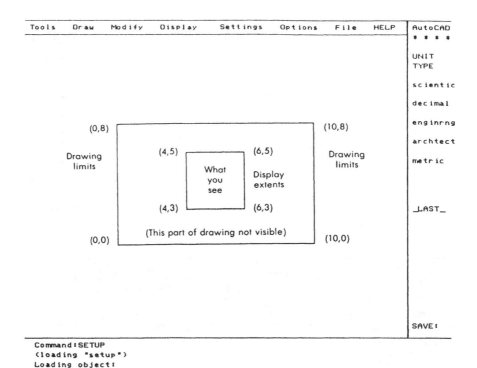

**Figure 4.4**  Loading SETUP from side menu.

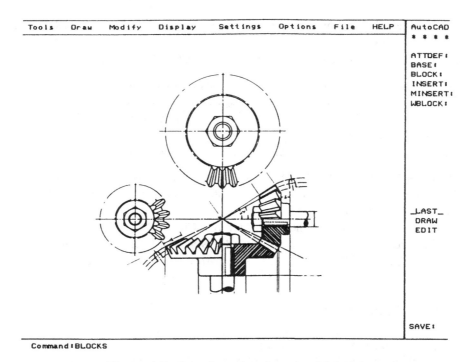

**Figure 4.5** Inserting a drawing using BLOCKS.

2.  CONSTANT. The attribute of the block of images has a fixed value, and unlike variables, cannot be changed later.
3.  VERIFY. If a group of images are formed into a block with this mode on, you have a chance during the insertion (creation) process to check that it is correct.

You may also enter I (invisible), C (constant), or V (verify) to reverse the yes–no response for the three modes described above. You may have the text describing the block (group) of images aligned (left), centered (middle), fit to size and styled to please, or placed on the right side of the image display. Once all this has been done, the prompt reads

```
Attribute tag:
```

which means that you may not enter the text that describes the graphics grouping.

Figure 4.5 shows what happens when BASE: is selected from the BLOCKS root menu. You must supply a *base insertion point* to be used by the INSERT menu items. This is a reference point when inserting the group of images into a new drawing format.

Figure 4.5 also shows what happens when BLOCK: is selected from the BLOCKS item from the root menu. This feature lets you create new blocks on the fly, as shown in Chapter 2. Notice that the subcommands allow you to "window," use the last item, select the previous image, indicate crossing group selection, remove items, and add items that appear graphically on the screen. You may need to review GROUP and UNGROUP at this time.

Figure 4.5 can also show what happens when INSERT: is selected:

```
Command: INSERT Block name (or ?): (type in name desired)
Insertion point: (point block image is to be placed)
X scale factor <1>/corner/XYZ: (number or data of point)
Y scale factor <X>: (data point desired)
Rotation angle <0>: (amount of image rotation counterclockwise)
```

Figure 4.5 indicates the MINSERT: submenu item. In Chapter 3 we used the ARRAY command to draw several objects. MINSERT: allows you to insert multiple copies of a block of graphic images.

Figure 4.5 is the final submenu item for BLOCKS and stands for "write block to disk." This creates a new drawing automaticaly. Notice that the editing commands from GROUP and UNGROUP can be used to save part of the drawing screen to WBLOCK.

## 4.4 DIM: Menu Item

Two types of dimensioning menus are provided as shown in Figure 4.6 and 4.7. DIM: contains a submenu LINEAR, as demonstrated kin the graphics are of Figure 4.6. The submenu items are: horizontal, vertical, aligned, rotated, baseline, and continued.

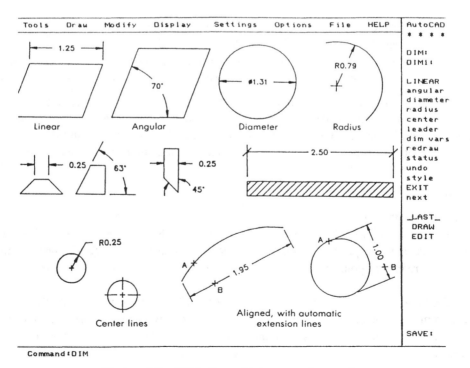

**Figure 4.6**   DIM: from side menu and examples.

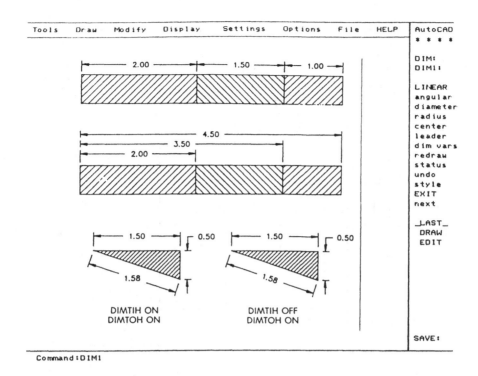

**Figure 4.7**  DIM1 from side menu and examples.

Continue the familiarization with menus by selecting DIM1:. Does your screen look like Figure 4.7? Practice the use of these menus by building the example graphics displayed in Figures 4.6 and 4.7.

## 4.5  DISPLAY Menu Item

Select the menu item and return to the root menu. Select the DISPLAY menu item and compare the listing with that shown in Figure 4.8. Each of these has a submenu. ATTDISP is used in the normal, on, or off modes. Normally, attributes are visible unless they are defined with the invisible mode on (see Section 4.3). The ATTDISP command allows you to override the state of visibility using

```
Command: ATTDISP
Normal/On/Off<default>:
```

PAN lets you view portions of a very large drawing without changing the magnification

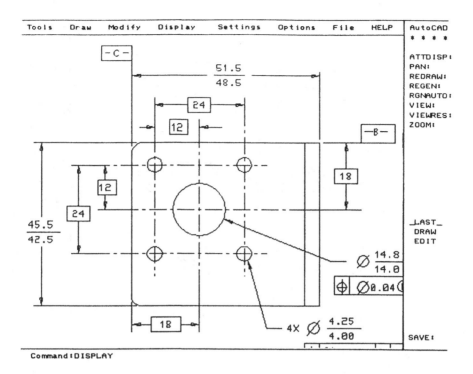

**Figure 4.8**   DISPLAY from side menu and WBLOCK.

(ZOOM). This lets you see portions that are not presently on the screen. To use this command, let's move the current screen contents shown in Figure 4.9 left, right, up, and down by

```
Command: PAN Displacement: -2, -3
Second point: (R)
```

This moves the drawing contents left 2 units and down 3 units.

   A REDRAW may be used to clean up a drawing under development. We used this command in Chapter 3. Its structure is

```
Command: REDRAW
```

REGEN can be used in place of REDRAW and forces the software to regenerate the entire drawing file .DWG to redraw the screen. This is therefore a much longer process than a simple REDRAW command. The RGNAUTO command stands for "automatic regeneration" of the drawing file. .DWG and the software prompts

```
About to regen, proceed<Y>
```

A "no" response will abort the PAN or ZOOM function.

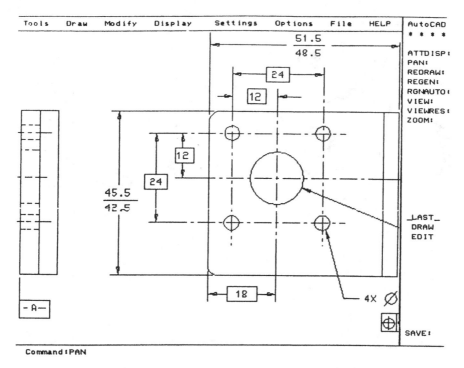

**Figure 4.9** PAN from side menu and WBLOCK.

The VIEW command is used as

```
Command: VIEW ?/Delete/Restore/Save/Window: (select one)
View name:
```

The ? produces a list of the named views currently known for this drawing, showing their names, center points, and magnifications. The delete option removes a view from the list of saved views. The restore replaces the current display on the screen by performing a ZOOM center. The save is used to store the drawing contents for use later. The window option allows you to assign two points, which describe the lower left and upper right corners of the window space. In Chapter 3 we showed you how to use it on the current screen locations by

```
Command: ZOOM
All/Center/Dynamic/Extents/Left/Previous/Window?<Scale(X)>: A
```

where A = show entire drawing surface
      C = ask for center point and height
      D = zoom and pan graphically by pointing
      E = shows current drawing extents
      L = lower left corner and height

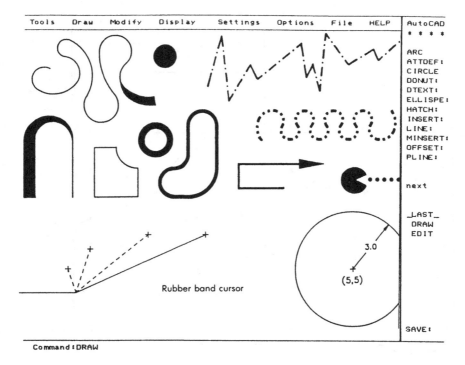

**Figure 4.10**   DRAW from side menu with several examples.

P = restores previous view
W = asks for rectangle to be enlarged or reduced
S = numeric magnification factor

## 4.6 DRAW Menu Item

FIgure 4.10 shows the DRAW menu and several examples of draw items displayed in the graphics area. The techniques are an expansion of Chapter 3. Figure 4.11 shows the DRAW and DIM commands used to create a drawing. For example, there are eight possible ways in which to draw arcs:

1. *Three point:* the default method of arc specification; the first and third points are the end points; for example:

```
Command: ARC Center/<Start point>:7,4
Center/End/<Second point>: 6,5
End point: 6,3
```

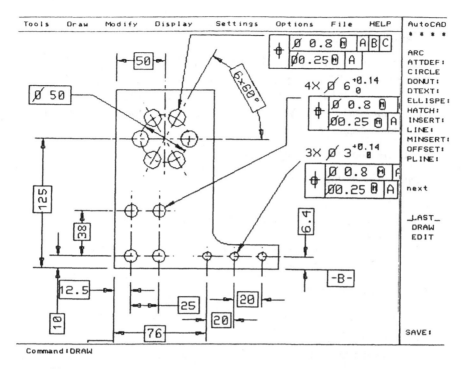

**Figure 4.11**   DRAW and DIM commands used to create a drawing.

2. *Start, center, end:* specifies an arc drawn counterclockwise from the start to the end with a center point.
3. *Start, center, included angle:* counterclockwise arc from start point, radius from center, and spanning the angle indicated.
4. *Start, center, length of chord:* counterclockwise arc from start point, radius from center, and with a length of chord printed out for you.
5. *Start, end, radius:* displays the minor arc counterclockwise from the start point; use a minus value for the major rac.
6. *Start, end, included angle:* counterclockwise arc if positive vaules are given, clockwise if negative values are given.
7. Start, end, starting direction: used to construct arcs tangent to another entity (circle, line, arc).
8. *Line/arc continuation:* a special case in which you respond with an (R) at the first prompt; the arc's start point and direction are taken from the end point and ending direction of the last arc or line drawn.

There are five methods for drawing circles:

1. *Center, radius.* The default method:

```
Command: CIRCLE 3P/2P/TTR/<Center point>: 5,5
Diameter/<radius>: 2
```

2. *Center, diameter.* Enter D and you select the diameter.
3. *Two point.* 2P lets you specify the circle as two end points.
4. *Three point.* 3P lets you specify a third point for the circle.
5. *Tange, tangent, radius.* You may select two entities for the tangent relationship and radius desired for the circle.

There are four methods for drawing an ellipses:

1. *Center.* This is the default:

```
Command: Ellipse
<Ax is endpoint 1>/Center:
Axis endpoint 2:
<Other axis distance>/Rotation:
Rotation around major axis:
```

2. *Rotate.* After the prompt

```
<Other axis distance>/Rotation
```

you may enter an R for "rotate."

3. *Iso.* After the prompt

```
<Axis endpoint 1>/Center
```

you respond with I for "Isocircle."

4. *Diameter.* Used only with isometric circles.


## 4.7   EDIT Menu Item

Figure 4.12 is the main menu listing for EDIT and some examples of commands such as ARRAY and BREAK. These menu items have been demonstrated in Chapters 2 and 3.

Notice that most of the submenus contain the same listings: window, last, previous, crossing, remove, add, and undo. Each of these was demonstrated in Chapter 2. Review how these editing techniques are used before continuing with the next section.


## 4.8   INQUIRY Menu Item

Figure 4.13 shows the root menu sublistings for INQUIRY. There are three types of submenus: editing (windows, last, etc.), ID (point locations), and no sublistings. Those items with no sublistings—DBLIST, DIST, HELP, STATUS, and TIME—are all direct AutoCAD commands and result in graphics to text screen outputs. Point locations in three dimensions are demonstrated in Chapter 5, and editing commands were covered in Chapter 2.

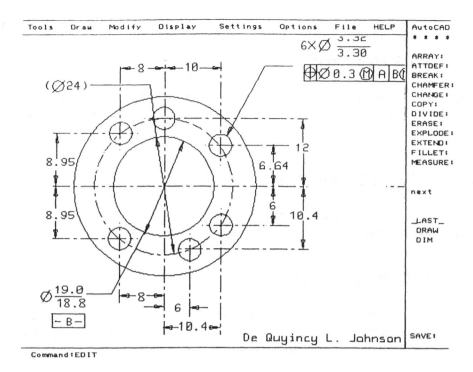

**Figure 4.12** EDIT from side menu used with WBLOCKS.

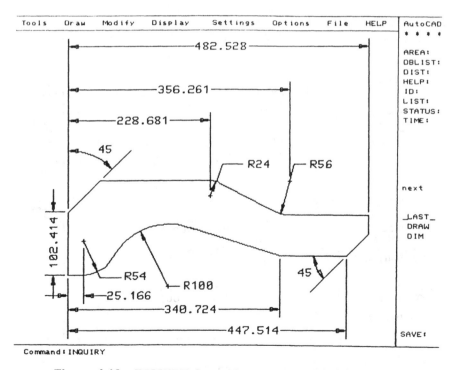

**Figure 4.13** INQUIRY from side menu used with WBLOCKS.

## 4.9   LAYER Menu Item

Figure 4.14 shows the listing from the root menu for LAYER:. The concept of layers was introduced in Chapter 3 and may be reviewed for use in this chapter by studying the figure.

## 4.10   SETTINGS Menu Item

Figure 4.15 is the root menu listing and demonstrates the items that need to be reviewed from Chapters 2 and 3.

## 4.11   UTILITY Menu Item

The UTILITY/PLOT menu selection from the tablet is shown in Figure 4.2; Figure 4.16 is the screen listing for UTILITY. The separate submenu listings are listed here. See later chapters for working demonstrations of each of these items.

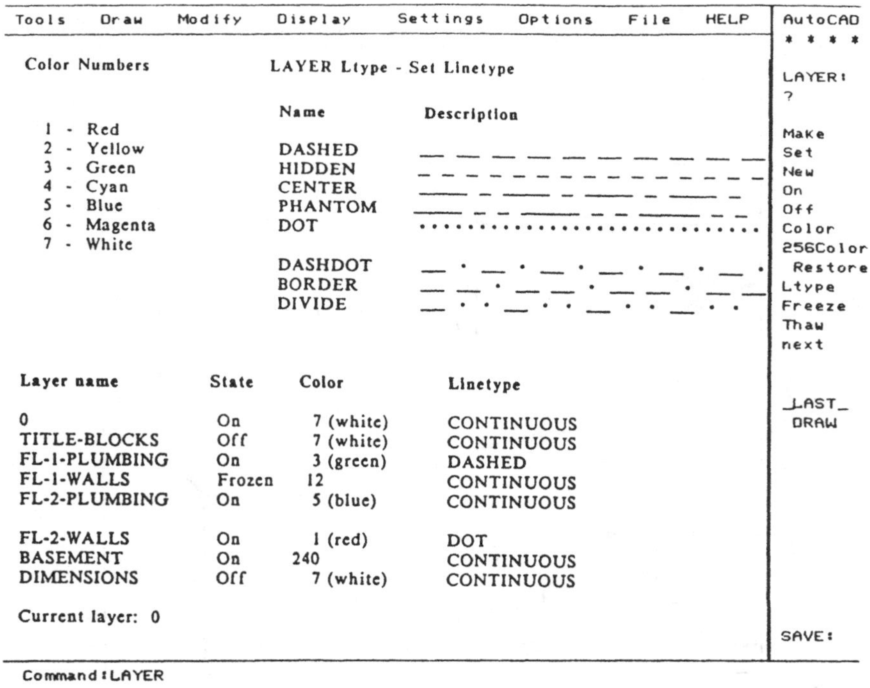

**Figure 4.14**   LAYER: from side menu.

Tools Draw Modify Display Settings Options File HELP
AutoCAD
* * * *
APERTUR:
AXIS:
BLIPS:
COLOR:
DRAGMOD:
ELEV:
GRID:
LINETYP:
LIMITS:
LTSCALE:
OSNAP:
QTEXT:
next
__LAST__
DRAW
EDIT
SAVE:
BASE (0,0)
BASE POINT
Object snap
Normal grid
Rotated & offset
A
B
C
Before
After
AXIS ruler lines
Screen menu
Command:SETTINGS
Prompt area

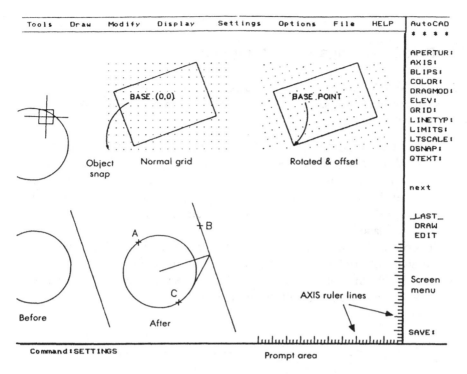

**Figure 4.15** SETTINGS from side menu.

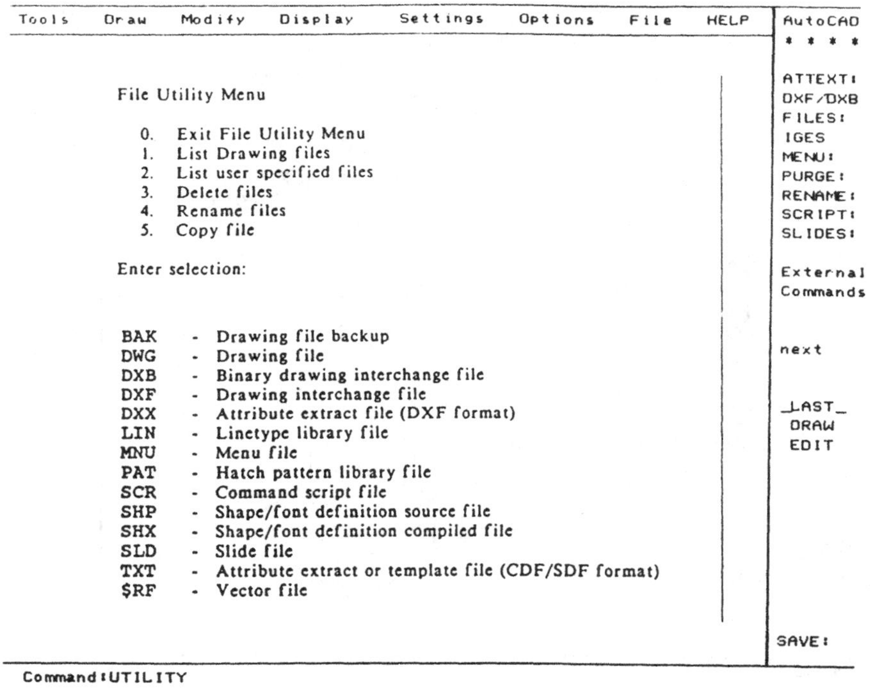

Tools Draw Modify Display Settings Options File HELP
AutoCAD
* * * *
ATTEXT:
DXF/DXB
FILES:
IGES
MENU:
PURGE:
RENAME:
SCRIPT:
SLIDES:
External Commands
next
__LAST__
DRAW
EDIT
SAVE:
File Utility Menu
0. Exit File Utility Menu
1. List Drawing files
2. List user specified files
3. Delete files
4. Rename files
5. Copy file
Enter selection:
BAK - Drawing file backup
DWG - Drawing file
DXB - Binary drawing interchange file
DXF - Drawing interchange file
DXX - Attribute extract file (DXF format)
LIN - Linetype library file
MNU - Menu file
PAT - Hatch pattern library file
SCR - Command script file
SHP - Shape/font definition source file
SHX - Shape/font definition compiled file
SLD - Slide file
TXT - Attribute extract or template file (CDF/SDF format)
$RF - Vector file
Command:UTILITY

**Figure 4.16** UTILITY from side menu.

## 4.12 Detail Drawings from Menu Items

Figures 4.17 to 4.20 are all examples of detail drawings completed by using the menu items just demonstrated. Using the menu items, the procedure for making a detailed drawing is as follows:

1. Select the views, remembering that in Chapter 3 the horizontal view was described by plotting the X and Y array from the DATAPT list. The other views are then rotated into position using conventional orthographic projection. In Chapter 5 you will be introduced to viewport selection. This procedure is recommended for large numbers of detailed drawings that need to be filed in an office situation.
2. Choose a drawing scale that will allow an arrangement of the views and the locations of needed dimensions, notes, and parts labels.
3. Call out the location for centerlines of features such as holes, slots, or machined sections and block in all fillets and rounds.

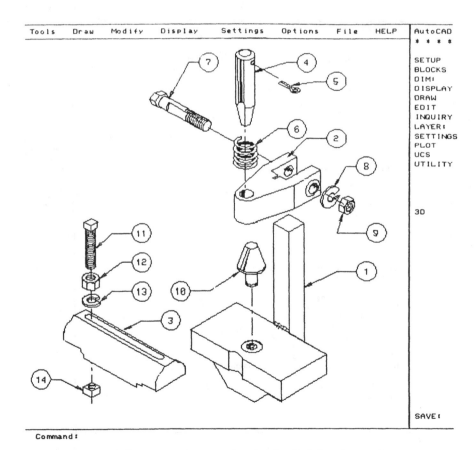

**Figure 4.17**  Assembly drawing for detailed drawing package.

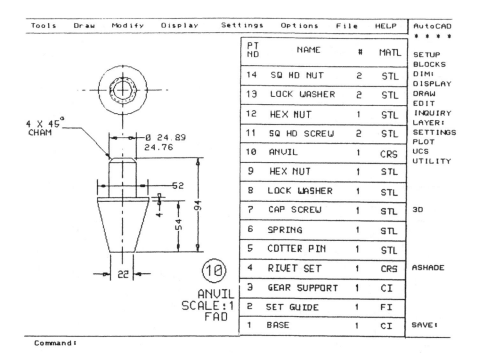

**Figure 4.18** Parts list and part number 10.

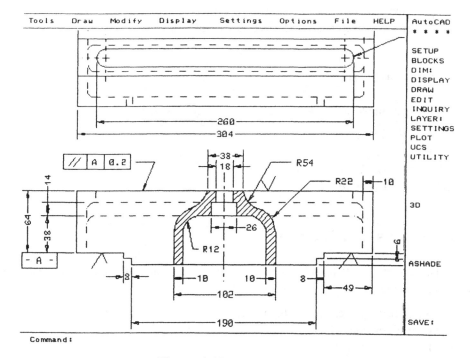

**Figure 4.19** Part number 3.

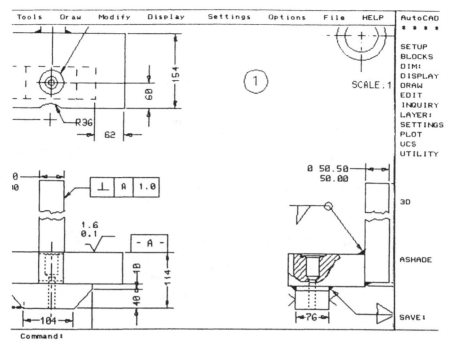

**Figure 4.20**   Part number 1.

4.  Add the dimensions as demonstrated earlier in this chapter.
5.  Select the proper notes and place them with DTEXT.

## 4.13   Sectional Views

The following example of sectional views have been provided:

1.  Full (Figure 4.21)
2.  Half (Figure 4.22)
3.  Broken-out (Figure 4.23)
4.  Revolved (Figure 4.24)

## 4.14   Threads and Fasteners

Using the sectional view techniques, the following examples of threads and fasteners have been provided:

1.  Simplified and schematic (Figure 4.25)
2.  Metric notations (Figure 4.26)
3.  Detailed (Figure 4.27) and
4.  Assemblies (Figure 4.28)

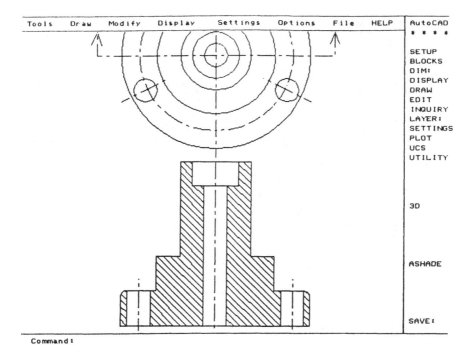

**Figure 4.21**  Full section.

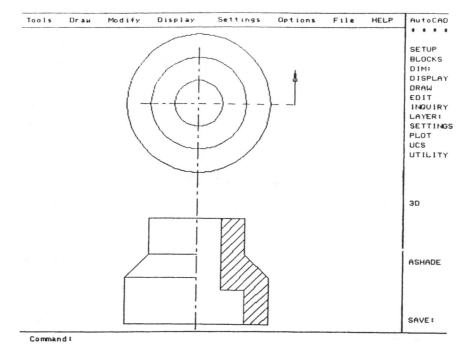

**Figure 4.22**  Half section.

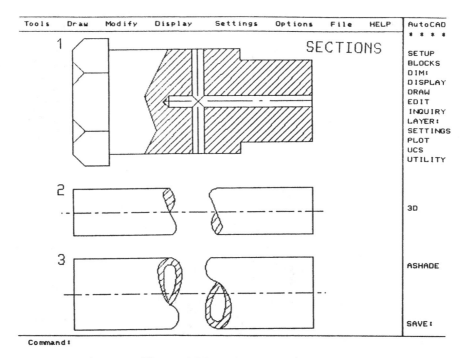

**Figure 4.23**   Broken-out section.

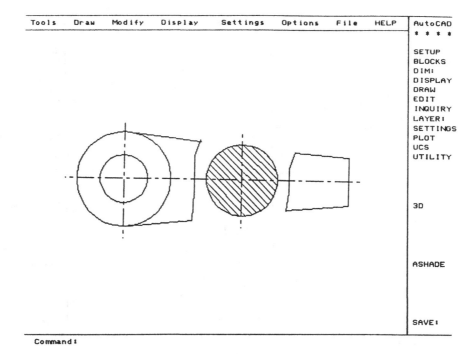

**Figure 4.24**   Revolved section.

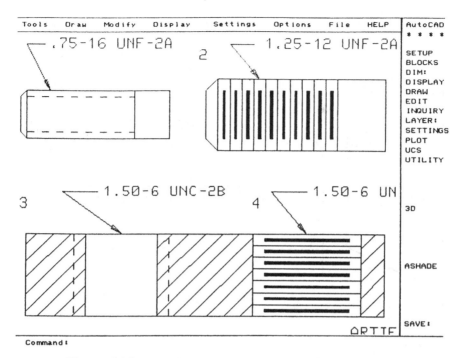

**Figure 4.25** Simplified and schematic thread representation.

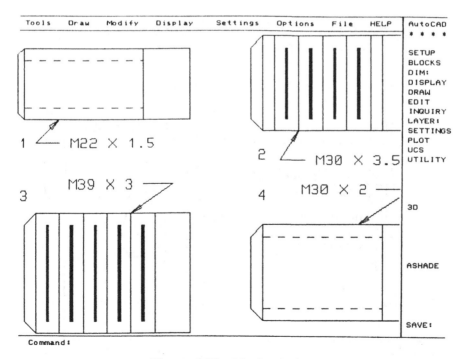

**Figure 4.26** Metric notation.

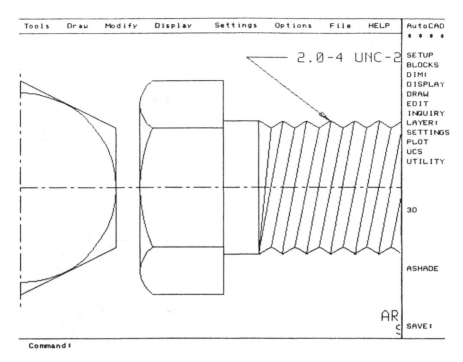

**Figure 4.27**   Detailed thread representation.

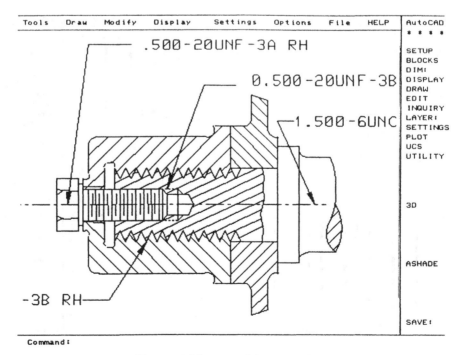

**Figure 4.28**   Assembled fasteners.

## Exercises

Try to simulate each of the following display screens.

1.

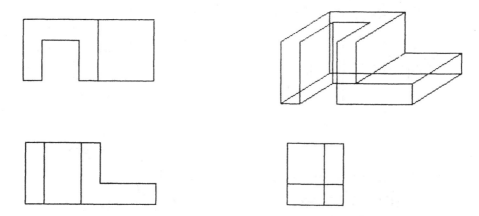

2.

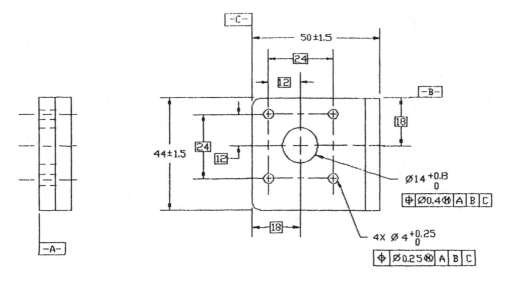

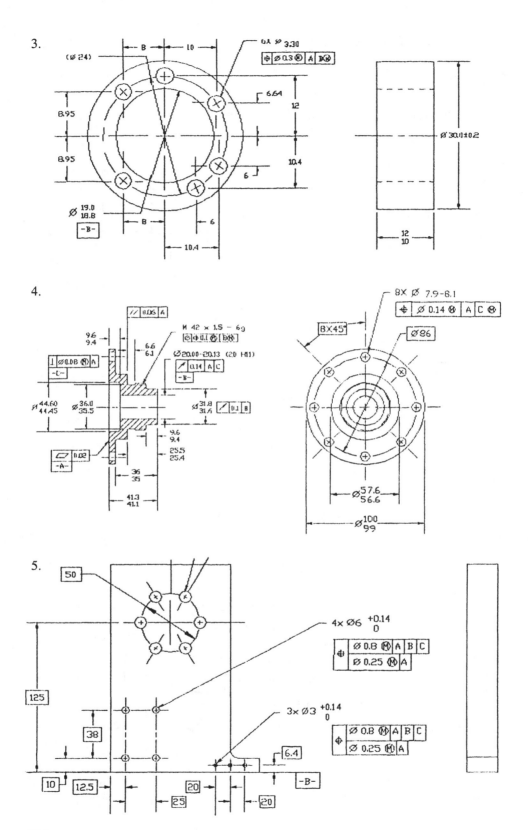

3.

4.

5.

6.

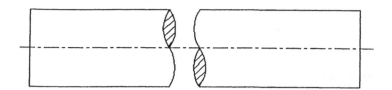

7.

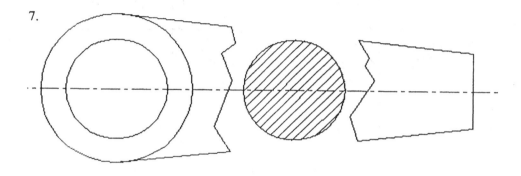

8.

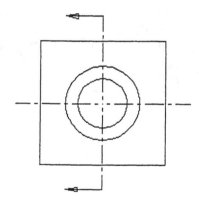

9.

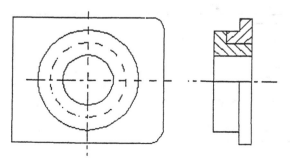

10.

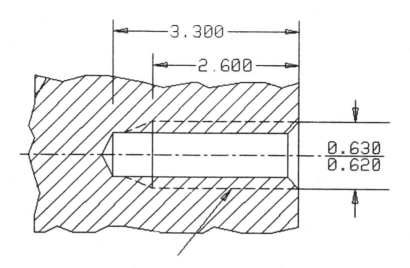

11.

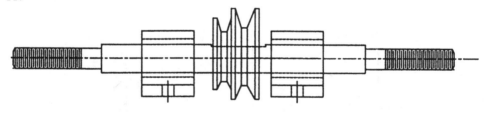

12.

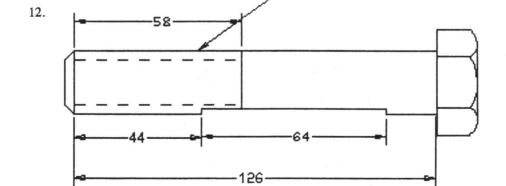

# 5

# Pictorial Representation

Earlier we discussed the importance of plane surfaces in CADD. This two-dimensional database was used to present everything from working views to planes used as cutting edges to expose the interior of a three-dimensional object. The creation of the pictorial representation was not presented. In this chapter we present the use of points, lines, and plane surfaces to construct pictorial objects. When a surface from a boundary completely enclosing a portion of space in three dimensions, it becomes a solid. The term *solid* is used in its mathematical sense. A mathematic solid is considered to be hollow. It is the wireform container for the object described. A solid is displayed as its edges and is completely described by the projections of these edges as a model, shown in Figures 5.1 to 5.3. Most graphic workstations are capable of solid displays in a variety of options. The options available for Autodesk software presentation include the following:

1. Wireform in any axonometric orientation (VPOINT command); shaped poylgon surfaces can be added to simulate halftones (AutoShade).
2. Solid models with hidden-line removal in any axonometric rotation.
3. List source for realistic model shades and shadows.
4. Primitives for cube, cone, pyramid, sphere, and torus (Figure 5.7).

With these options, realistic solids that have surprising detail can be displayed. AutoSolid and AutoShade software are part of the Autodesk format used throughout this book.

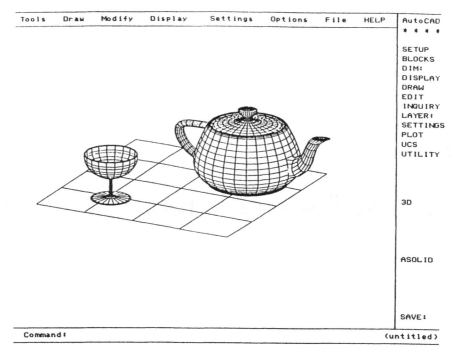

**Figure 5.1** Mathematical solids.

## 5.1 Solid Definition

In this chapter we describe the use of solids as defined within the Autodesk software AutoLISP. This denotes theoretical solids and has the same meaning as in ANSI Y14.5M; therefore, solid descriptions will represent a basis for an object from which permissible variations may be established by augmenting physical characteristics. Geometric descriptions (Figure 5.1) include solid building blocks consisting of points, lines, curves, and surfaces to define the solid. Topological descriptions cover the pertinent connectivity relationships for the solid. The information structure within AutoLISP and explained in this chapter is a language format that anticipates the need to associate nongeometric data with various levels of object shape data for solids.

## 5.2 Information Structures

The information structure within AutoLISP is a machine-and human-readable language with a well-defined syntax. The unit of information employed here may be one of the following:

1. Domain
2. Geometric

3. Topological
4. Miscellaneous

A domain structure defines a set of solid data in terms of its members, which are a finite collection of numerical values or character strings representing attributes. This structure is particularly useful in terms of extensibility into the areas of product definition data for CADD. The geometric structure describes geometric entities (point, line, plane, or solid combinations) used to construct a solid. Methods used to construct solids are interpolation, generation, point-set operations, replications, and a small selection of special operations. Topological structures define relationships among vertices, edges, faces, and objects in terms of their interior boundaries. These structure are built from simple to more complex entities.

## 5.3 Solid Entities

Three classes of entities are used to create solid: geometric, topological, and miscellaneous. Geometric and topological haev just been defined; miscellaneous entities are composed of only the GROUP entity, which is a collection of other entities (smaller solid subparts). A collection of entities described through the same structure type is known as a *relation*. A relation is communicated as shown in Chapter 3 for a plane surface.

A plane represents a relation for a linear blend (interpolation) of points that come from specified domains. These data may be expressed in a language format as

```
PLANE/LIN/ENT0,ENT1,PNTA,PNTB:P1(P1,P2,P3)
```

The parameter data for a plane may be shown as follows:

| Parameter | Value | Format | Comment |
|---|---|---|---|
| 1 | n | I | Number of points in plane |
| 2 | ie | I | Pointers used in plane surface to show order of connections |
| 3 | m | I | Number of properties for plane |
| 4 | rel | A | Language format used |

The parameter data for a solid may be shown as follows:

| Parameter | Value | Format | Comment |
|---|---|---|---|
| 1 | n | I | Number of lines in the boundary |
| 2 | ie | I | Pointers used in solid edges to show order of connections |
| 3 | m | I | Number of properties (surfaces) for the solid |
| 4 | rel | A | Language format used (AutoLISP) |

A linear view of the parameter data for a plane is

| AutoLISP | DIR entry |
|---|---|
| Lines | Relation entity, name, and pointer |

```
PLANE/LIN/ENT0,ENT1/POINTS,POINTS:
P1(P1,P2,P3)
```

A linear view of the parameter data for a solid is

| AutoLISP | DIR entry |
|---|---|

Edges             Relation entity, name, and pointer
```
LINES/LIN/ENT0/ENT1/POINTS,POINTS,POINTS:
S1(P1,P2); L2(P2,PE) ........ LN(Pn,Pn+1)
```

Figure 5.1 represents the Autodesk display for a solid as a linear blend (interpolation) of points that come from specified domains. A better understanding of communication of language format via file structure can be seen from an Autodesk example as in Figure 5.2. The edges of a solid are displayed in a connected format. This type of screen display is called the *wireform* of the solid.

The completed solid statements for Figure 5.2 are shown displayed in Figure 5.3, and a portion of the relational table format is shown in Figure 5.4. A file structure portion is shown in Figure 5.5, and a sample portion of the linear file format is shown in Figure 5.6. Where solid generation is used, it is generally explained in context. However, the software generation provided in Figure 5.7 is used throughout this chapter.

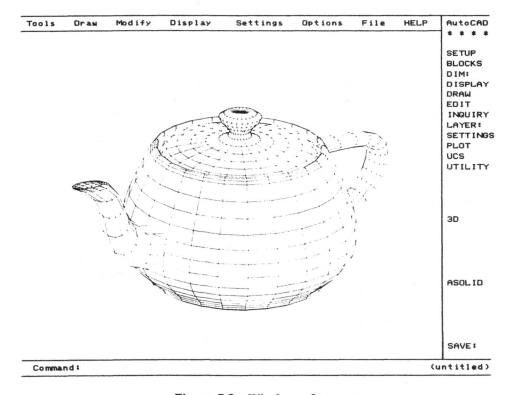

**Figure 5.2** Wireform of a teapot.

Command:                                                        (teapoted)

**Figure 5.3**   AutoShaded surfaces for TEAPOT.

| Tools | Draw | Modify | Display | Settings | Options | File | HELP | AutoCAD |
|-------|------|--------|---------|----------|---------|------|------|---------|
| | | | TEAPOT | | PNTR001 | | | * * * |
| | | | | | | | | SETUP |
| | POINTS | | X | Y | Z | | | BLOCKS |
| | | | | | | | | DIM: |
| | P1 | | 0. | 1. | 0. | | | DISPLAY |
| | P2 | | 0. | 2. | .185 | | | DRAW |
| | P3 | | .185 | 0. | 0. | | | EDIT |
| | P4 | | 1. | 2.250 | 0. | | | INQUIRY |
| | . | | | | | | | LAYER: |
| | . | | | | | | | SETTINGS |
| | . | | | | | | | PLOT |
| | P77 | | 0. | 0. | 7.500 | | | UCS |
| | | | | | | | | UTILITY |

PNTR001:  '77 POINTS'

| | | TEAPOT | | ENTR001 | | | |
|---|---|--------|---|---------|---|---|---|
| LINES | | ENT0 | | ENT1 | | | 3D |
| G1 | | P1 | | P2 | | | |
| G2 | | P2 | | P3 | | | |
| G3 | | P3 | | P4 | | | |
| . | | | | | | | ASOLID |
| G139 | | P47 | | P77 | | | |

ENTR001:  '139 LINES'

SAVE:

Command:                                                        (untitled)

**Figure 5.4**   Relational table format for TEAPOT.

**121**

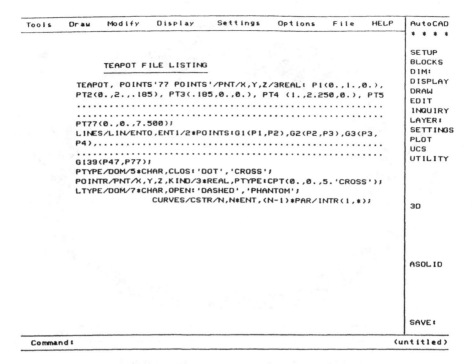

**Figure 5.5** File structure for TEAPOT.

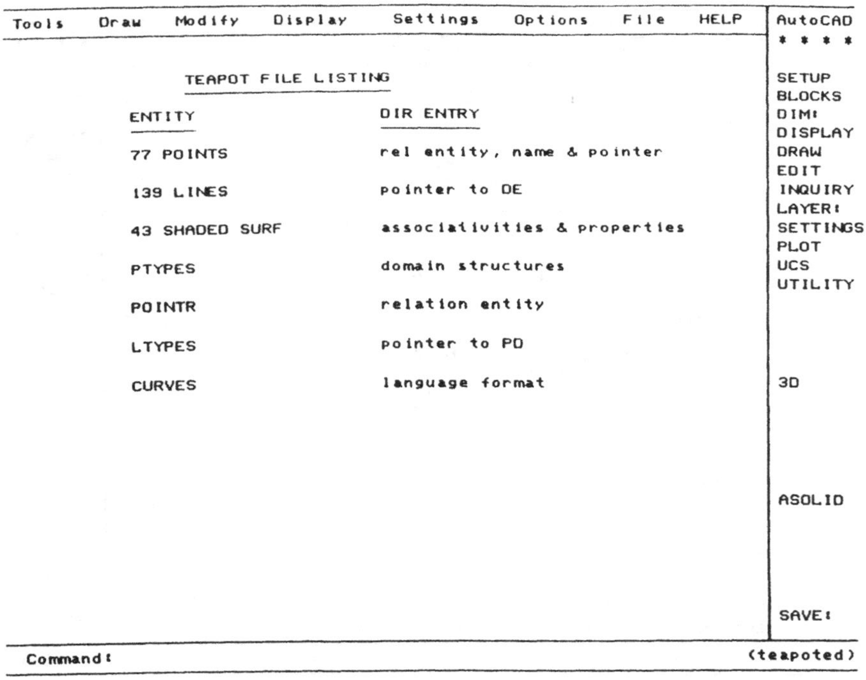

**Figure 5.6** Linear file for TEAPOT.

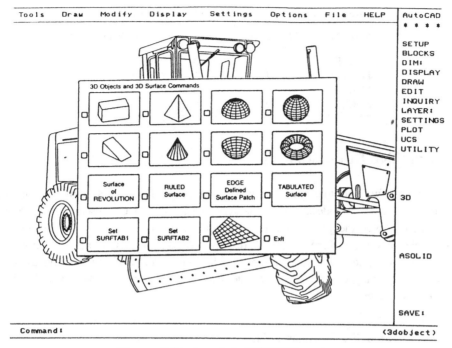

**Figure 5.7** Autodesk OBJECTS menu.

## 5.4 Geometric Structures

The geometric structure describes the shape and mathematical representation of the solid defined. The solids specified in this chapter are divided into six classes:

1. Primitive
2. Interpolative
3. Generative
4. Special
5. Point set
6. Replicative solids

These solids are displayed constructively, with the primitive structure being the basic building blocks.

The primitive, interpolative, generative, and special solids are displayed as parametric entities; that is, the entities are displayed as images of I(n), for n = 0, 1, 2, or 3, under a continuous function. I(n) is called the parameter space and the parameters are named u,v,w; Table 5.1 relates these concepts to dimension and entity type. Table 5.2 lists all the geometric structures possible. The point-set and replicative structures are not parametric but are displayed as transformations represented by entities.

**Table 5.1** Dimensionality and Parameterization

| Structure | Dimension | Space | Parameter |
|-----------|-----------|-------|-----------|
| POINT | 0 | 0 | 0 |
| LINES | 1 | 1 | u |
| SURFACES | 2 | I(2) | (u,v)′ |
| SOLIDS | 3 | I(3) | (u,v,w) |

## 5.5  Primitive Structures

From Table 5.2 we note that point and marker, shown in Figure 5.8, comprise the only two such structures. Autodesk uses a marker system called UCS (user coordinate system), which defines the precise location of solid geometry in space. The origin of a UCS can be placed anywhere within the display area, and the UCS axes can be rotated or tilted at any angle, as shown in Figure 5.8. The location of the viewing axes are shown by the display of a small coordinate system icon, shown in the lower left-hand corner of the screen.

**Table 5.2** Geometric Structures

| Structures | Solid | Surface | Line | Point |
|------------|-------|---------|------|-------|
| Primitives | | | | |
| Point | — | — | — | ✓ |
| Marker | — | — | ✓ | — |
| Interpolative | | | | |
| Line | — | — | ✓ | — |
| Arc | — | — | ✓ | — |
| Cubic | ✓ | ✓ | ✓ | — |
| Nth-degree poly | ✓ | ✓ | ✓ | — |
| Spline | ✓ | ✓ | ✓ | — |
| Generative | | | | |
| Translation | ✓ | ✓ | ✓ | — |
| Rotation | ✓ | ✓ | ✓ | — |
| Special | | | | |
| Reverse | — | — | ✓ | — |
| String | — | — | ✓ | — |
| Flip | — | ✓ | — | — |
| Point set | | | | |
| Closure | ✓ | ✓ | ✓ | ✓ |
| Union | ✓ | ✓ | ✓ | ✓ |
| Intersection | ✓ | ✓ | ✓ | ✓ |
| Difference | ✓ | ✓ | ✓ | ✓ |
| Replicative | | | | |
| Translation | ✓ | ✓ | ✓ | ✓ |
| Rotation | ✓ | ✓ | ✓ | ✓ |
| Scale | ✓ | ✓ | ✓ | ✓ |
| Mirror | ✓ | ✓ | ✓ | ✓ |

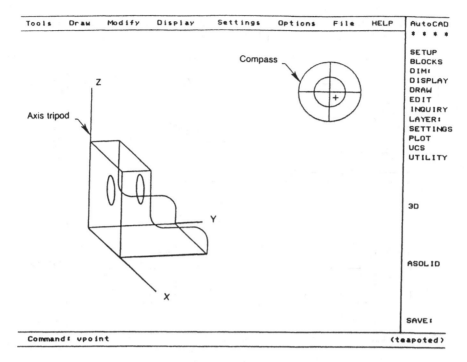

**Figure 5.8**  Primitive point and marker system.

## 5.6  Primitive Symbols

The UCS icon is shown in Figure 5.9 as it would be seen from various viewpoints. A W displayed in the Y arm indicates that the current UCS coincides with the world coordinate system. If a + appears at the lower left of the icon, it indicates that the icon itself is located at the UCS origin point. Autodesk may also display the UCS icon as a special symbol. When the X-Y plane of the current coordinate system is perpendicular to your viewing plane, a broken pencil inside a box is displayed. This is to indicate that selecting and drawing solids is limited in such a situation.

The icon is positioned by the VPOINT command. Refer to Figure 5.9, view port 3, to see the result of Vpoint (0,1,1); view port 2 contains (1,-1,1); view port 1 contains (0,0,0). The VPOINT command also provides an option allowing you to specify a three-dimensional viewpoint in terms of two angles: one within the X-Y plane of the current UCS measured counterclockwise from the X axis, and other one measured up from the X-Y plane. View port 4 contains the result of

```
Command: VPOINT
Rotate/<view point> <current>: R
Enter angle in the X-Y plane from X axis <current>: 30
Enter angle from the X-Y plane <current>: 50
```

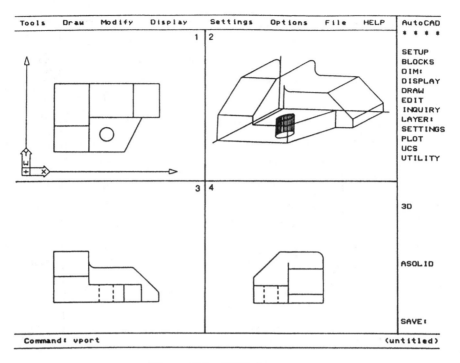

**Figure 5.9**   UCS placement.

## 5.7   Interpolative Structures

From Table 5.2 we see that line, arc, cubic, Nth polynominal, and spline are all interpolative. Further study of display figures will indicate how Autodesk statements are used to display each figure. For example, Figure 5.10 shows three examples of line interpolation, used to create a three-dimensional (3D) polygon mesh of a surface entity defined by a matrix of 3D vertices. You can specify as many as 256 vertices in two directions and thus control the density or tabulations of the mesh to suit your solid application. The examples shown in Figure 5.10 consist of 100 vertices, 10 in one direction and 10 in the other direction.

Three-dimensional meshes are typically used to display partial sections of a solid model. These sections are then joined together to develop a complete model (Figure 5.11). Several methods are available in Autodesk software to generate interpolative structures. To demonstrate, a series of display figures will illustrate each method listed in Table 5.2. In Autodesk software, you can create a display figure by one of the following:

1.   Indicating the position of each vertex in the mesh using the 3DMESH command
2.   Creating edge geometry and interpolating a surface by using a TABSURF, RULESURF, REVSURF, or EDGESURF command

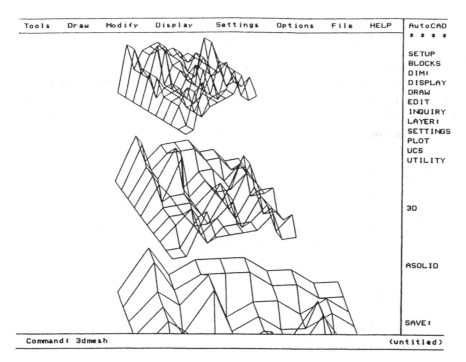

**Figure 5.10**  Line interpolation (3D examples).

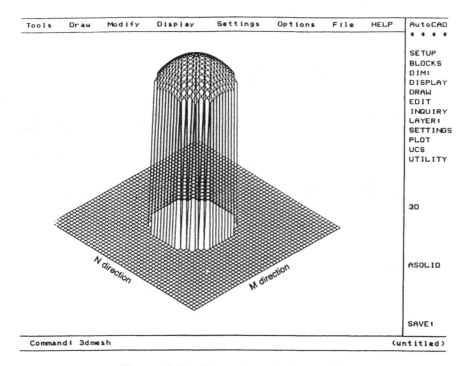

**Figure 5.11**  Linear interpolation model.

3. Placing control points and approximating a surface about the control points by using either a quadratic, cubic, or bezier approximation.

These techniques are demonstrated first in Figure 5.12, where a vertex-by-vertex mesh is defined in the M and N directions. This display was begun with a matrix of 3D points. Although point entities are not needed to define a 3D mesh, they are provided here to make the selection of each vertex in the mesh easier. You may display a similar mesh by following the prompts in this chapter section to select a "running" example called NODE.

```
COMMAND: OSNAP
OBJECT snap modes: NODE
```

When you enter the 3DMESH command, Autodesk will ask for the M and N size of the mesh. Let's say that we want the M direction to be the horizontal direction and the N direction to be the vertical. Enter the following prompts:

```
COMMAND: 3DMESH
Mesh M size: 5
Mesh N size: 4
```

So the M size is 5 and the N size is 4. After the mesh size is specified, you may input

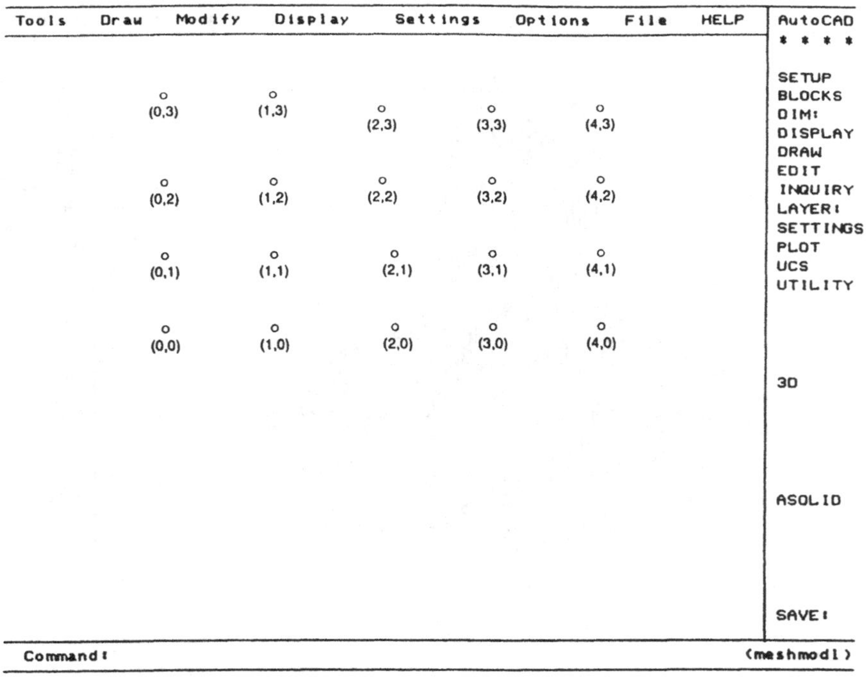

**Figure 5.12**   M and N point matrix.

vertex locations as follows:

> Vertex (0,0): pick point 1 shown in Figure 5.13
> Vertex (0,1): pick point 2
> .          continue to pick points
> .
> .
> .
> .
> .
> Vertex (4,3): pick point 20

After you have picked each location as shown in view port 1 of Figure 5.13, a mesh is displayed for you. To get a better view of the mesh, view port 2 has been set to

```
COMMAND: VPOINT
Rotate/<View Point> <0.0,0.0,1.0>:
Enter angle in X-Y plane from X axis <270>:315
Enter angle from X-Y plane <0.,>:15
```

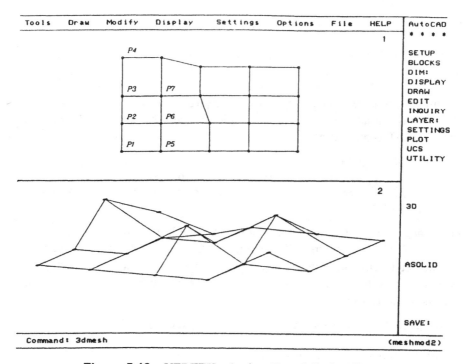

**Figure 5.13**   VERTEX selection (1) and display (2).

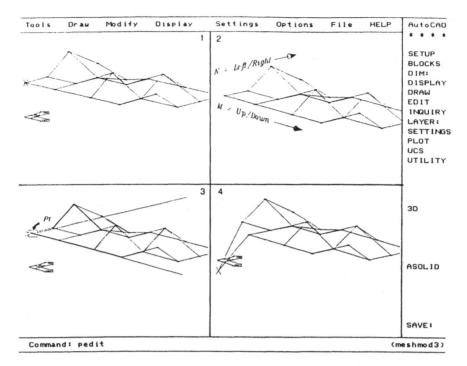

**Figure 5.14**   PEDIT to change 3DMESH output.

The display you have created can be moved, copied, rotated, or scaled just as any other display entity. In addition, the vertices within the mesh can be moved individually using the PEDIT command as

```
COMMAND: PEDIT
Select   polyline:    <pick mesh on display screen>
Edit vertex/Smooth surface/Desmooth/Mclose/Nclose/Undo/
  eXit/<X>:
```

Let's change the 3D location of a vertex in the mesh as shown in Figure 5.14, view ports 1 to 4. Respond to the PEDIT prompt with E and an "x" is displayed as shown in view port 1. This is the vertex to change. View port 2 shows how the "left/right/up/down" options will be used, view port 3 shows the pick box for point 1, and view port 4 shows the results of

```
Vertex (0,0). Next/Previous/Left/Right/Up/Down/REgen/
  eXit<N>:M
Enter new location:-2
```

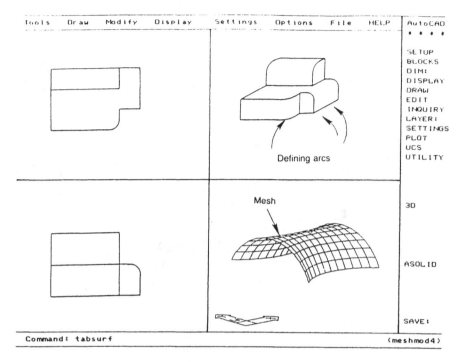

Tools  Draw  Modify  Display    Settings   Options   File   HELP   AutoCAD

Defining arcs

Mesh

Command: tabsurf                                                    (meshmod4)

**Figure 5.15**   ARC interpolation using TABSURF.

## 5.8   ARC Interpolation

An arc-defined mesh is a mesh displayed from existing interpolation geometry. For example, the curved surface in Figure 5.15 is interpolated between four arcs created previously. Although arc-generated meshes have M and N directions just like line meshes, the mesh size is specified differently. Two Autodesk variables called SURFTAB1 and SURFTAB2 are used to control the density.

## 5.9   CUBIC Interpolation

A cubic-defined solid is a solid displayed from existing interpolation geometry. For example, the curved solid in Figure 5.16 is interpolated between display points created previously from an equation. The cubic method of interpolation is intended primarily to be used to create application-specific solids with AutoLISP in a language-based format.

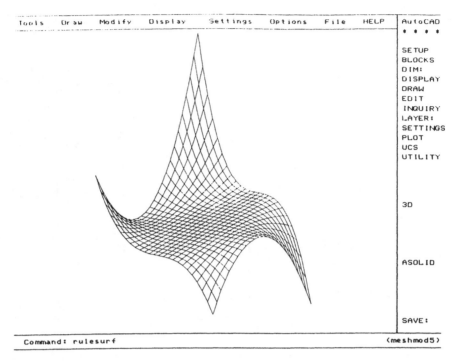

**Figure 5.16** CUBIC interpolation using RULESURF.

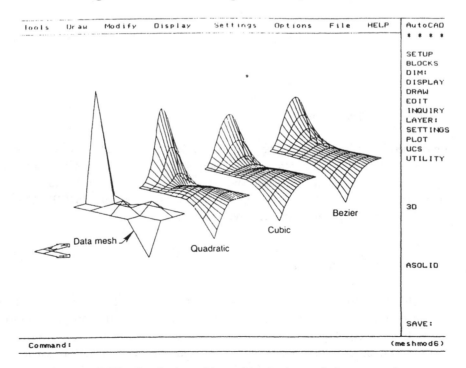

**Figure 5.17** Quadratic, cubic, and bezier interpolation comparison.

## 5.10   Approximate Interpolations

A cubic-defined solid is one of three approximations provided by Autodesk. Quadratic and bezier are also available. Each type of approximation will display a slightly different surface for a solid, as shown in Figure 5.17. The system variable SURFTYPE 5 will select quadratic, SURFTYPE 6 will select cubic, and SURFTYPE 8 will select Bezier.

## 5.11   Generative Structures

A generative structure requires the ability of translate and rotate images in the creation of the solid. Autodesk provides two commands: REVSURF, shown in Figure 5.18, and RULESURF, shown in Figure 5.19. The REVSURF command generates a surface of revolution by sweeping a profile path around a rotation axis. The path curve can be a 2D or 3D polyline, line, arc, or circle. The density of the surface mesh is controlled by setting SURFTAB1 (M) and SURFTAB2 (N) as

```
COMMAND: REVSURF
Select path curve:
Select axis of revolution:
Start angle <180.>:
Included angle (+=ccw,-=cw)<450.>:
```

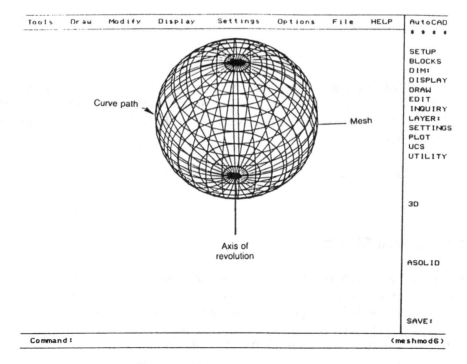

**Figure 5.18**   REVSURF example.

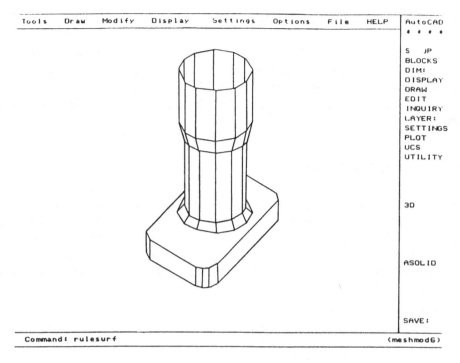

**Figure 5.19**   RULESURF example.

The RULESURF command generates a surface of straight tabulation lines translated along two path curves, with the end points of the tabulation lines touching the path curves at specified intervals. The surface swept out by the lines creates a ruled surface mesh for the solid as

```
COMMAND: RULESURF
Select first defining curve:
Select second defining curve:
```

## 5.12  Special Structures

From Table 5.2 we note that four types of structures are used to orient solids. These are not used to display or build solids but are used to view solids. Autodesk provides the DVIEW command for this purpose. This allows the dynamic previewing of parallel or perspective views of solids through the use of slider bars. This command uses a CAMERA and TARGET to relate the DVIEW options to the solids.

You may practice the use of DVIEW with any saved solid object that you have created. The object of this example is to view the solid from different 3D viewpoints to get a better idea of how a solid is constructed. We will use DVIEW to specify target and camera points, change the view from the ground level to above the solid object, and walk around the solid dynamically.

```
Enter the DVIEW command and "window" the object when
  prompted:
COMMAND: DVIEW
Select objects: w
Other corner:

CAmera/TArget/Distance/POints/PAn/Zoom/TWist/Hide/Undo/
  <eXit>:PO
Enter target point<
```

The CA (camera) option allows you to rotate the camera point dynamically around the target. The CA point can be specified in terms of two angles, similar to the VPOINT command's ROTATE option. The first angle rotates from the X-Y plane, and the second rotates around the target point. The CA also allows you to preview what the resulting view will look like as you chose the two angles. When you enter the CA option, Autodesk displays a slider bar at the right of the screen. As you move the cursor within the slider bar, all the objects you selected when you entered the DVIEW command will be visible as you rotate the camera around the target point. After the first angle is selected, another slider bar appears at the top of the screen, allowing you to select the second angle dynamically.

The D option allows perspective viewing. Selecting the perspective view entails two elements, the D option and the focal length of the lens of the camera. You can type in the distance or select it from a slider bar. You can adjust the focal length of the lens by selecting the Z option. This allows you to adjust your field of view by asking for a length specified in millimeters. A small lens length increases your view angle and creates the effect of looking at a solid with a wide-angle lens.

To practice the other options of DVIEW, type OFF to get out of perspective and then you can try PAn (reposition the solid), TWist (rotate solid), Hide (drop wireform lines), Undo (delete last option), and eXit (leave DVIEW).

## 5.13 Point Set and Replicative

Four examples from Table 5.2 are displayed as Figures 5.20–5.23.

1. DVIEW examples (see Figure 5.20)
2. CAmera example (see Figure 5.21)
3. Dimension-selecting closure example (see Figure 5.22)
4. Unions (see Figure 5.23)

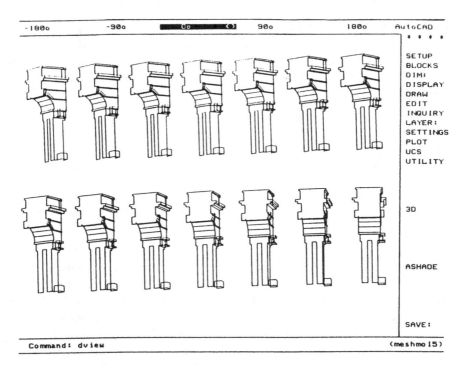

**Figure 5.20**   DVIEW example.

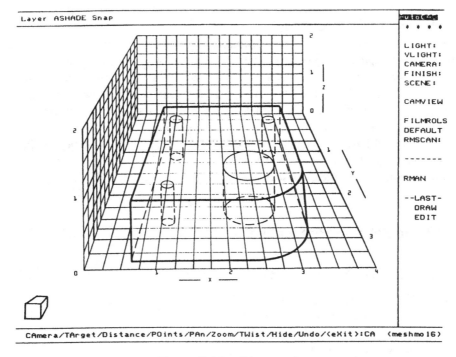

**Figure 5.21**   CA example.

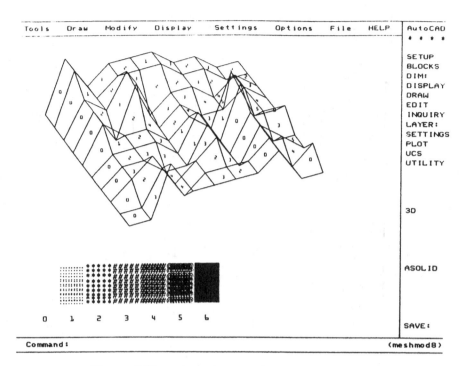

**Figure 5.22** Dimension-selecting closure example.

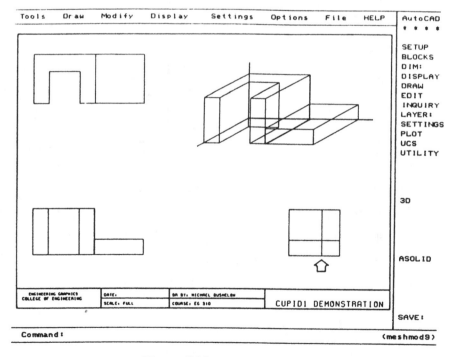

**Figure 5.23** Union example.

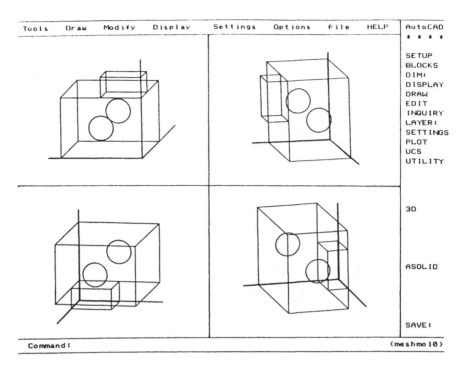

**Figure 5.24** Intersection example.

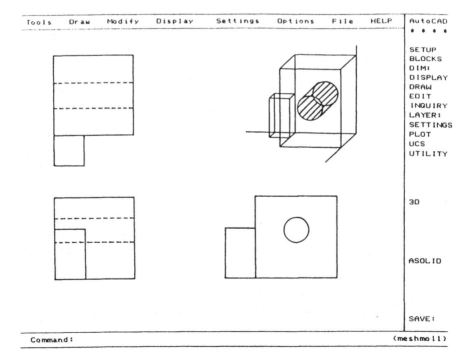

**Figure 5.25** Difference example.

**Table 5.3** Structure and Sense Preservation

| Replication | Preserves structure? | Preserves sense? |
|---|---|---|
| TRANSLATION/ROTATION | Yes | Yes |
| ROTATION | Yes | Yes |
| TRANSLATION | Yes | Yes |
| SCALE | No | Yes |
| REFLECTION | Yes | No |

## 5.14 Replicative Structures

Replicative structures define entities of the same dimensionality as the original. As these do not depend on a parameterization, they can be presented in data tables as shown in Tables 5.3 and 5.4 and in Figures 5.24 and 5.25.

## 5.15 Topological Structures

Topological structures provide a vehicle for representing various relationships that exist among geometric, replicative, and special entitites for solid constructions. The most useful of these are VERTEX (Figure 5.13), TABSURF (Figure 5.26), EDGESURF (Figure 5.27), and 3DFACE (Figure 5.28).

**Table 5.4** Replication Structures

| Replication | $T_1$ | $R_1$ | S | $R_2$ | $T_2$ | Input Triples | | | | | | |
|---|---|---|---|---|---|---|---|---|---|---|---|---|
| | | | | | | Q1 | Q2 | Q3 | R1 | R2 | R3 | K |
| TRANSLATION/ ROTATION | $\mathcal{T}_{-A_1}$ | $\mathcal{R}_\alpha{}^T$ | $I_4$ | $\mathcal{R}_\beta$ | $\mathcal{T}_{B_1}$ | √ | √ | √ | √ | √ | √ | X |
| ROTATION | $\mathcal{T}_{-A_1}$ | $\mathcal{R}_\alpha{}^T$ | $I_4$ | $\mathcal{R}_\beta$ | $\mathcal{T}_{A_1}$ | √ | √ | √ | =Q1 | =Q2 | √ | X |
| TRANSLATION | $\mathcal{T}_{-A_1}$ | $I_4$ | $I_4$ | $I_4$ | $\mathcal{T}_{B_1}$ | √ | X | X | √ | X | X | X |
| SCALE | $\mathcal{T}_{-A_1}$ | $I_4$ | $\begin{bmatrix} KX & & & 0 \\ & KY & & \\ & & KZ & \\ 0 & & & 1 \end{bmatrix}$ | $I_4$ | $\mathcal{T}_{A_1}$ | √ | X | X | X | X | X | √ |
| REFLECTION | $\mathcal{T}_{-A_1}$ | $\mathcal{R}_\alpha{}^T$ | $\begin{bmatrix} 1 & & & 0 \\ & -1 & & \\ & & 1 & \\ 0 & & & 1 \end{bmatrix}$ | $\mathcal{R}_\alpha$ | $\mathcal{T}_{A_1}$ | √ | √ | √ | X | X | X | X |

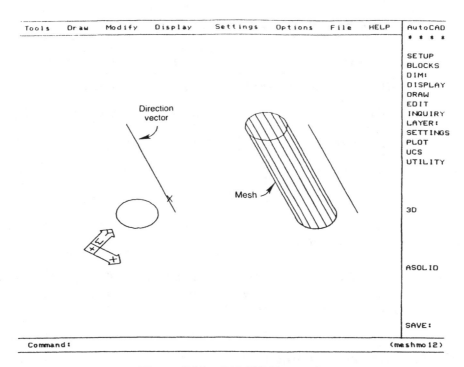

**Figure 5.26**    TABSURF example.

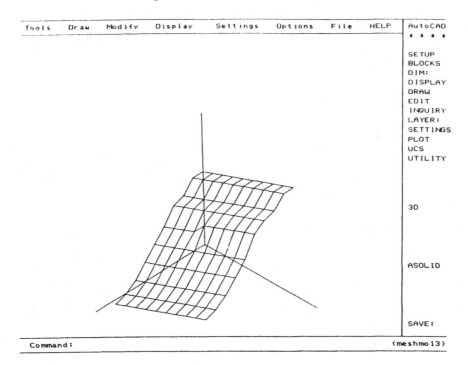

**Figure 5.27**    EDGESURF example.

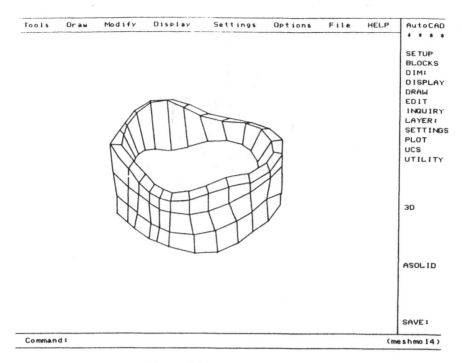

**Figure 5.28** 3DFACE example.

## 5.16 Exercises

Try to simulate each of the following display screens.

1. Wireform

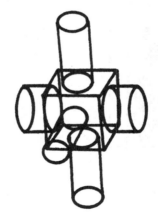

2.  Solid model

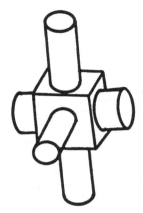

3.  Light sources

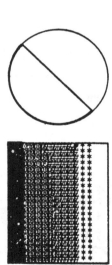

4. Primitives

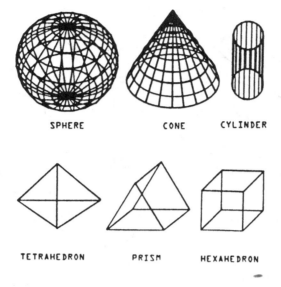

5. Interpolative

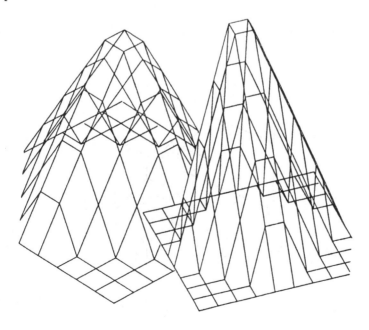

6. Generative

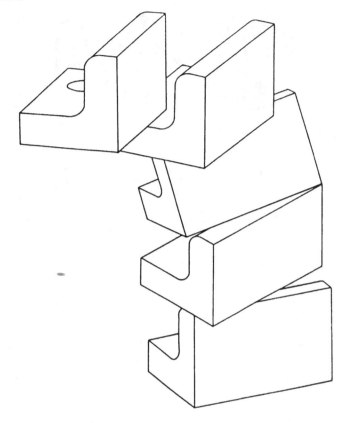

7. Special

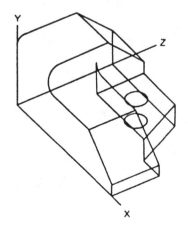

8. Point set

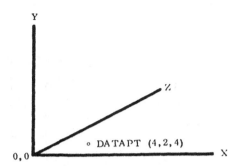

9. Replicative

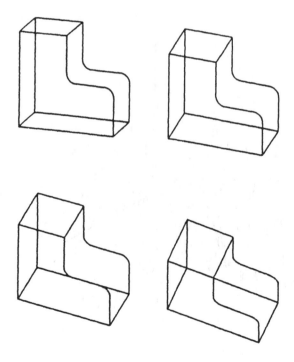

10.   Primitive structure

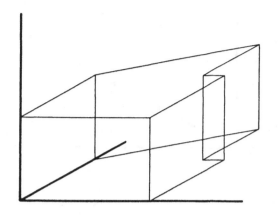

11.   3DMESH

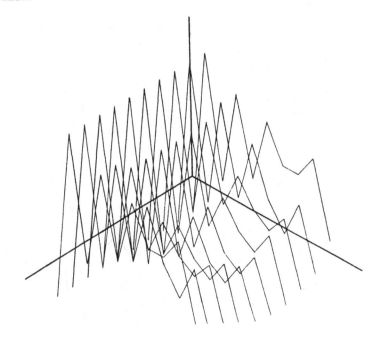

12. VPOINT

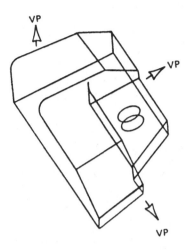

13. Arc interpolation

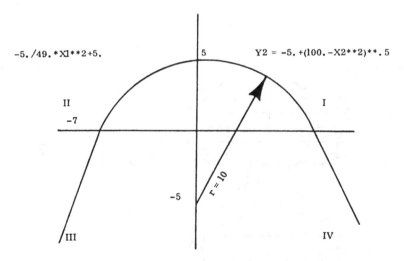

$-5./49.*X1**2+5.$

$5$

$Y2 = -5.+(100.-X2**2)**.5$

II

$-7$

I

$-5$

$r = 10$

III

IV

$/0./49.*X+10.$

$Y3 = -1.*3.**.5*X3+15.$

14. Cubic interpolation

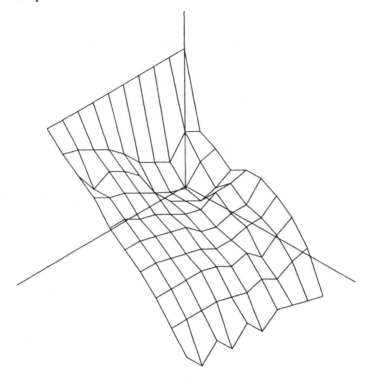

15. REVSURF

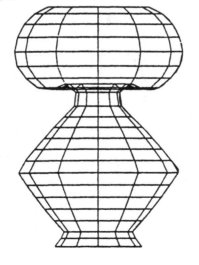

SURFTAB1 = 12
SURFTAB2 = 24

16. RULESURF

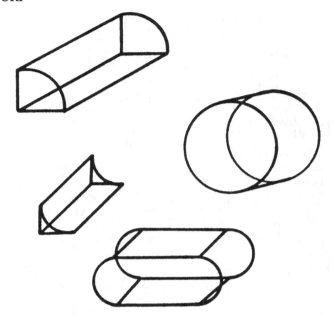

17. DVIEW

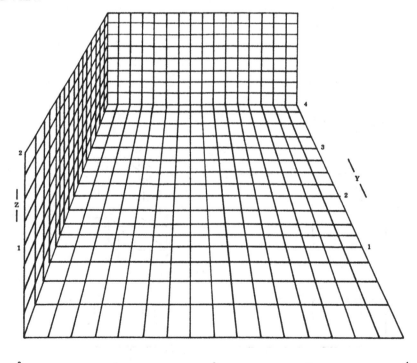

18.   CAmera

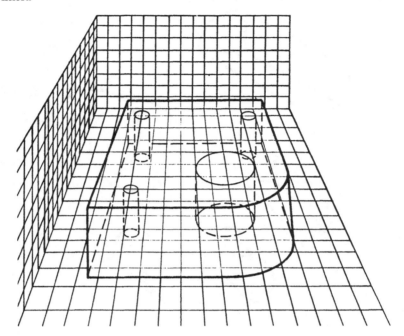

19.   Dimension selecting

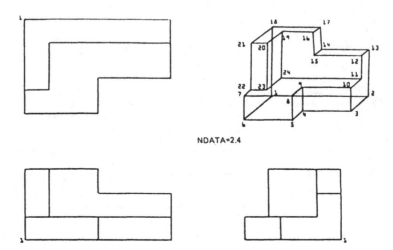

NDATA=2.4

20. Unions

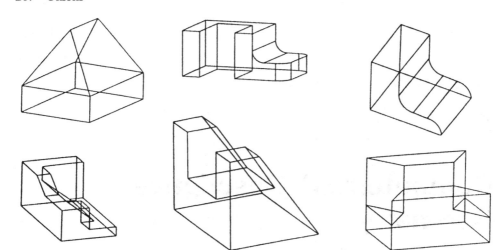

# 6

# Computerized Descriptive Geometry

Computerized descriptive geometry (CDG) is a mixture of plane geometry, third-quadrant orthographic projection, and CADD methods discussed in Chapters 1 to 5. In this chapter we introduce the fundamentals of each and the application of these CDG processes. For readers with some background, this chapter will appear slow paced. The topics covered in this chapter are for those who want a sound foundation in fundamentals.

CDG as we use it today evolved from the manual practice of the late nineteenth century into the electronic revolution of the late twentieth century and the use of CADD. Therefore, CDG is part of a design language and is used for one of the following purposes:

1. Image construction
2. Image maintenance
3. Creation of an industrial product or project (CAD)

We use CAD to produce industrial drawings of all types and descriptions.

## 6.1 CDG in the Design Process

The design process consists of several stages that mark the development of an idea into a product. A modified version of the design process is shown in Figure 6.1. It has been

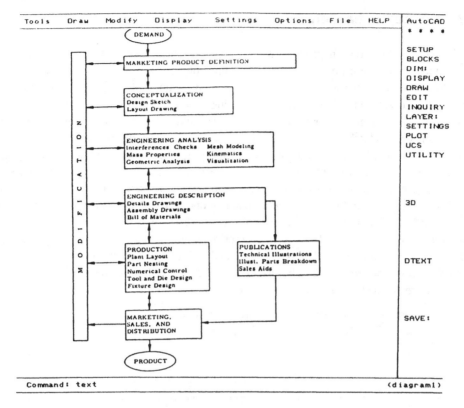

**Figure 6.1** CDG in the design process.

modified to better illustrate the areas where CDG plays an important role in communicating information.

The figures, diagrams, and monitor displays included in this chapter contain graphical symbols and a conventional system of line segments:

1. ━━━━━━━━  object lines

2. ─────────  construction lines

3. ─ ─ ─ ─ ─ ─ ─ ─  projection lines

4. ─ ─ ─ ─ ─ ─ ─  hidden lines

5. ──── ─ ────  centerlines, traces, rotation lines

6. ──── ─ ─ ────  axes of revolution, reference lines

7. ↑   ↑   ↑   ↑  direction of sight

## 6.2 Conceptualization

At this stage of the design process, the engineer begins to collect first impressions of the solution to a design problem. Most often this solution is based on past experiences. Therefore, the solution can be documented by modifications of past solutions stored in the CADD workstation. This situation of creating a new design by modifying an already existing design is a good candidate for CDG. The old solutions are retrieved, and the new features are added by editing a copy of the existing design. A layout can be constructed from the trial solution in memory. This is the most desirable stage of the design process at which to add information to the design database. The database uses a special system of unit measurement consisting of three reference planes.

These three mutually prependicular planes—one horizontal (HP) and two vertical (FP and PP)—are shown in Figure 6.2. These reference planes serve as the system of measurement or coordinate planes for the description and storage of points, lines, planes, and solids. These reference planes (HP, FP, and PP) intersect in the three axes labeled 0X, 0Y, and 0Z in Figure 6.2. The origin (0) is the intersection of the three axes. Four quadrants are formed by the intersecting axes:

1. Where X and Y measurements are both positive (+)
2. Where X is negative (−) and Y is positive

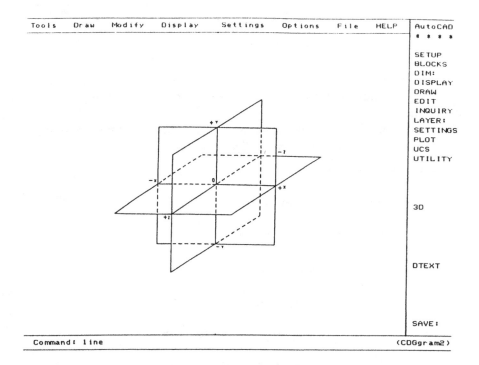

**Figure 6.2**   CDG coordinate system.

3. Where X is negative and Y is negative
4. Where X is positive and Y is negative

Measurements are made to points in one of three four quadrants where

X = distance to point right or left of 0, as +X or –X
Y = distance to point above or below 0 as +Y or –Y
Z = distance to point before or behind 0, as +Z or –Z

The point measurements (coordinates) are always given in X, Y, and Z order, and the distances are displayed in GDU (graphic display units). A graphic display unit is set at the CADD workstation and can be anything from SI (metric) to English feet and inches for architectural applications. For this chapter, the units of measurement are all in millimeters unless noted otherwise. So a point located at (25,50,75) is 1 inch (25 millimeters) to the right, 2 inches above, and 3 inches in front of the origin.

## 6.3 Engineering Analysis

After the creation of the database for the layout drawings, the designer will experiment with the design to determine its validity. One of these analyses is the geometric verification of points in space (how the design will fit together). This involves a determination as to whether the system of measurement described in Figure 6.2 can be used to define space in much the same way that a mathematician describes points in a plane system of measurement. In this chapter we shall see further similarities:

1. Parametric descriptions of a line in space are quite similar to an equation of a line in a plane.
2. Distance descriptions (true lengths) are a simple extension of the equation for the plane.
3. Planes in space can be described by the location of three or more lines.
4. Solids can be described simply by means of equations.

For this section we need to review the Euclidean postulates for space coordination.

**EP1.** There is a set (group) of points (real numbers, mapped as order triplets). Certain subsets (members of the group) are called lines; at least two points are needed to define a line. Certain other subsets are called planes; at least three points are needed to define a plane. Solids contain at least four points not in any one plane.

**EP2.** There is exactly one plane containing any three noncollinear points.

**EP3.** Each plane satisfies all other postulates.

**EP4.** Each plane separates space into half-spaces with the following properties:

1. If two points are in the same half-space subset, a line between them does not intersect the plane.
2. If two points are in different half-spaces, a line between them will intersect the plane.

From these few postulates all the theorems of modern descriptive geometry can be derived. However, we will not derive any theorems in this book. All that is required is an understanding of the elementary aspects of space geometry and the ability to visualize and display some space figures. In this regard you should observe that the CADD display problem is one of representing three-dimensional relations in a plane: namely, the monitor face. Planes will be displayed by plotting a parallelogram, suggesting a portion of a plane. Lines that are behind planes as viewed in Figure 6.2 are dashed (hidden).

## 6.4  Engineering Description

In Figure 6.3 we define a one-to-one mapping of ordered pairs of real numbers onto the points of the plane, so analogously, for space projection we define a one-to-one mapping of ordered triples or real numbers onto reference planes. These projections depend on certain choices:

1.  The projection of a point is the base of the perpendicular from the point to the reference plane as shown in Figure 6.3.

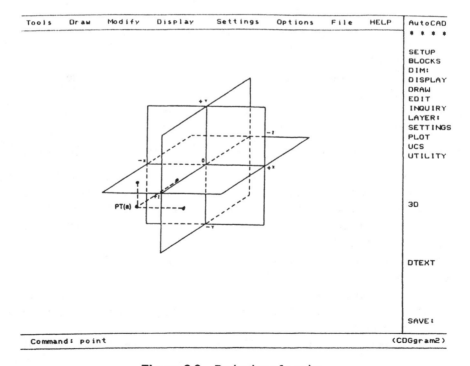

**Figure 6.3**  Projection of a point.

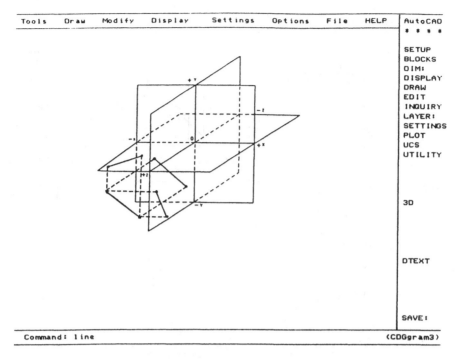

**Figure 6.4** Projection of a line.

2. The projection of a line is the locus of the projections of all points of the line on the reference plane, as in Figure 6.4.
3. The projection of a nonperpendicular line is a straight line as shown in Figure 6.4, while the projection of a perpendicular line is a point.
4. The projection of a line parallel to a reference plane is a straight line on the reference plane and equal in length to the given line (true length), as shown in Figure 6.5.
5. A projection of two lines such that a straight line joining any two of its points lies wholly between the two lines is called a *projected plane* (Figure 6.6).
6. If two points common to a plane are connected, the line lies wholly in that plane (Figure 6.7).
7. Points and lines lying in the same plane are said to be *coplanar*, while lines and points not sharing the same plane are called *noncoplanar* (Figure 6.8).
8. Lines common to the same plane must be either parallel or intersecting (Figure 6.9).

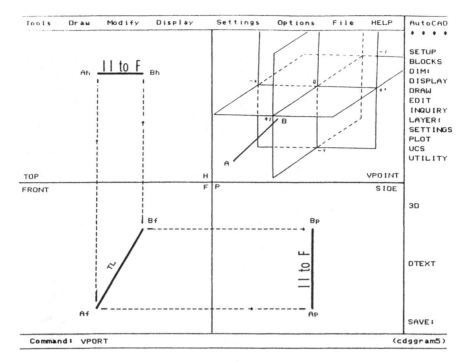

**Figure 6.5**   Parallel projection of true length.

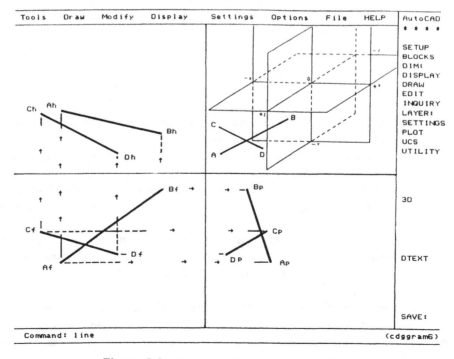

**Figure 6.6**   Projected plane between two lines.

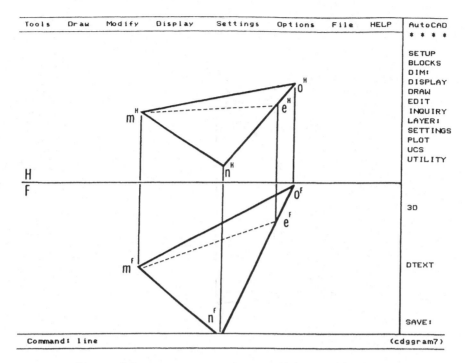

**Figure 6.7** Two points within a plane connected by a line.

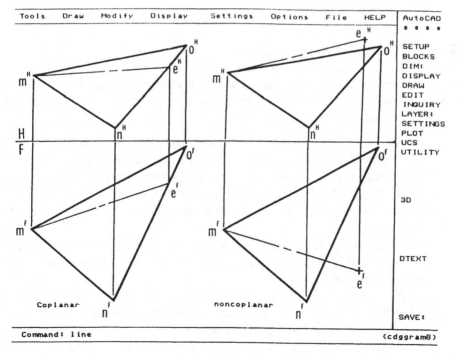

**Figure 6.8** Coplanar and noncoplanar line segments.

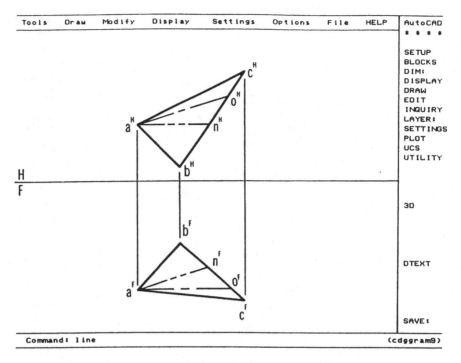

**Figure 6.9**   Lines common to the same plane.


## 6.5   Engineering Conventions

There are several conventions that are observed in coordinate space geometry. These conventions have to do with lines (parallel, intersecting, and perpendicular), planes, and solids. The following conventions apply:

1. *Parallel lines*. Coplanar lines that cannot intersect however far projected are called parallel lines (Figure 6.10). Through a given point, only one line can be displayed parallel to another. Two coplanar lines are parallel if both are perpendicular to a third coplanar line. Two lines parallel to the same line are parallel to each other. Finally, two lines perpendicular to the same plane are parallel to each other.

2. *Intersecting lines*. If two coplanar lines are not parallel, they must intersect, as in Figure 6.11. Two straight lines can intersect at only one point, called a *concurrent point* for both lines.

3. *Perpendicular lines*. Lines that intersect at right angles are called perpendicular. An infinite number of space lines can be displayed perpendicular to a given line, as in Figure 6.12. From a given point only one line can be displayed perpendicular, however. Only one line can be displayed perpendicular to two intersecting lines.

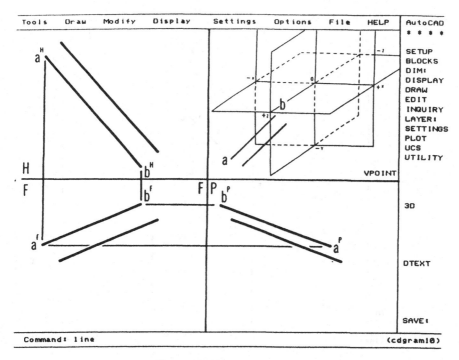

**Figure 6.10** Parallel lines.

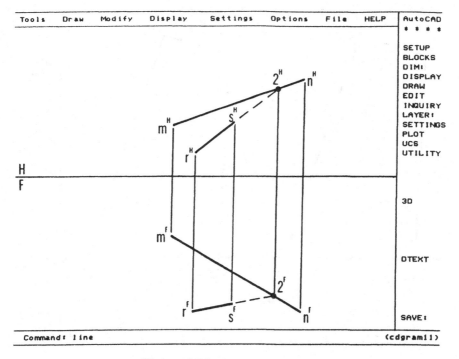

**Figure 6.11** Intersecting lines.

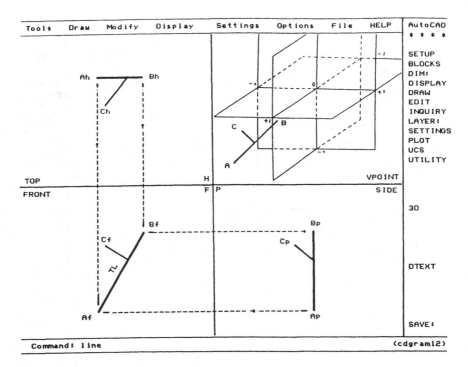

**Figure 6.12**   Perpendicular lines.

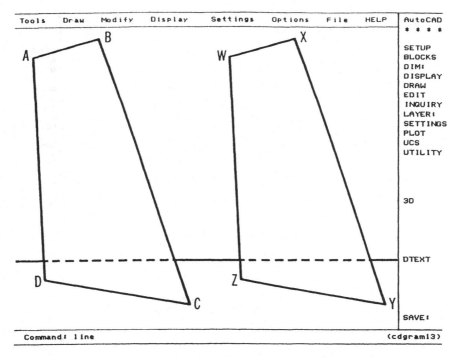

**Figure 6.13**   Parallel planes.

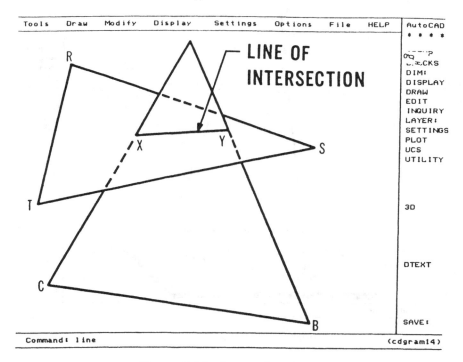

**Figure 6.14** Intersecting planes.

4. *Parallel planes.* Two planes are parallel if they cannot intersect, as in Figure 6.13. All of the conventions for lines apply to planes.

5. *Intersecting planes.* If two planes intersect, one line is concurrent. This concurrent line is the locus of all points common to the two planes, as in Figure 6.14. If three planes intersect, the lines of intersection are concurrent or parallel to each other. If a plane intersects two parallel lines, the lines of intersection are parallel.

6. *Perpendicular planes.* If a plane is perpendicular to a line in another plane, the two planes are perpendicular, as in Figure 6.15. If two planes are perpendicular, any line in one plane projected is perpendicular to any other.

7. *Parallel solids.* The planes forming a solid are called its *faces,* and their concurrency is called the *edge* of the solid. If a face of one solid is parallel to another face of a second solid, the solids are said to be parallel, as in Figure 6.16.

8. *Intersecting solids.* The intersection of two solids is a plane surface. This plane surface may be (1) a straight line and a point not in the line, (2) three points not in a straight line, or (3) two parallel lines, as in Figure 6.17.

9. *Perpendicular solids.* If a plane in one solid is perpendicular to a plane in another solid, the solids are considered to be perpendicular, as in Figure 6.18. In the case of intersecting solids, the dihedral angle between the faces of the solids must be 90°.

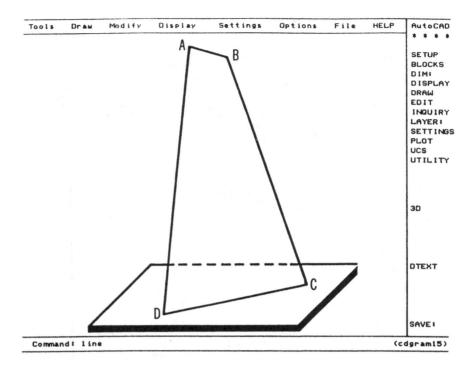

**Figure 6.15**  Perpendicular planes.

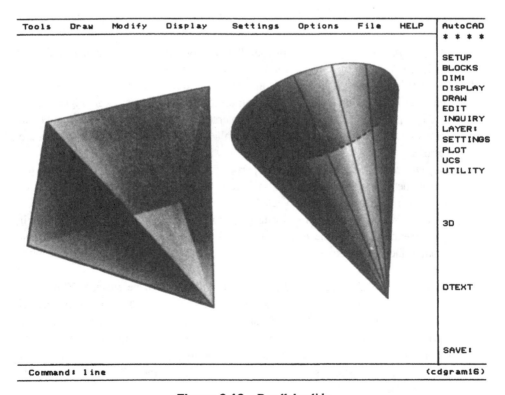

**Figure 6.16**  Parallel solids.

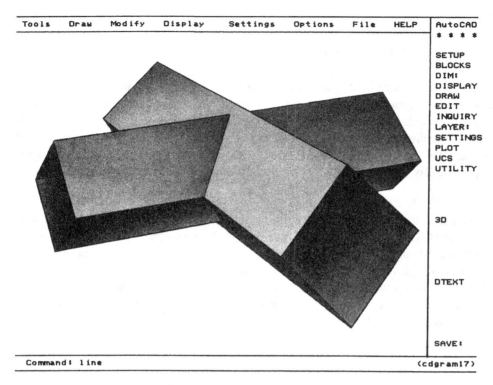

**Figure 6.17** Intersecting solids.

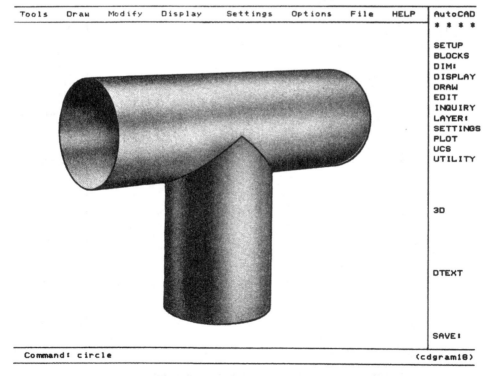

**Figure 6.18** Perpendicular solids.

165

## 6.6   Points Used in Production

We have defined euclidean space and have given it coordinates. But often, in the applications of mathematics to problems of engineering production, it is the converse situation that prevails. We are given ordered triples of real numbers and use space to illustrate graphically the relations between the ordered triples. In some cases there is no need to chose the display option. Often, the CADD workstation has only one method for graphic display, as in Figure 6.19. In most systems a point (PT) is simply

PT $(a_1, a_2, a_3)$

Furthermore, there is no definite way to orient the display axes, but it is customary to default the CADD display so that X is horizontal, Y is vertical, and Z is in and out of (perpendicular to) the display screen, as in Figure 6.20. For observation purposes you may position and reposition the display axes at will. The three coordinate planes shown in Figure 6.2 separate display space into eight octants. Usually, only one of them is given a name; this is the first octant, which consists of the sets of all points having positive coordinates only, and this is stated as

PT $(x_1, y_1, z_1)$

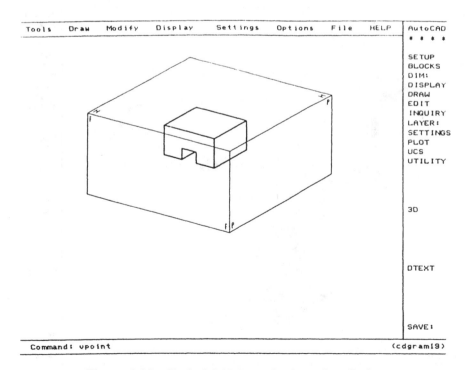

**Figure 6.19**   Typical CADD production points display.

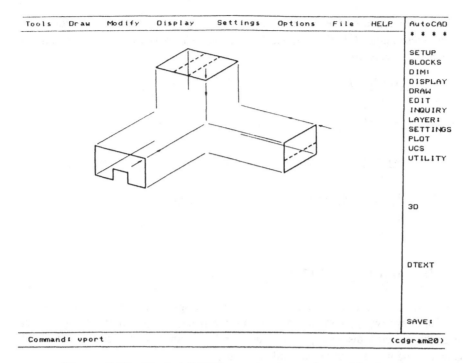

**Figure 6.20** Typical CADD mapping into orthographic views.

## 6.7 Production Distances

We are provided the two points PT(1) = (X(1),Y(1),Z(1)) and PT(2) = (X(2),Y(2),Z(2)). If we chose to add point 3 so that points 1 and 3 have the same Z value, the distance |PT1PT3| is given by the equation in the plane:

$$|PT1PT3| = ((X(1)-X(2))**2+(Y(1)-Y(2))**2)**.5 \qquad (1)$$

The points PT2 and PT3 are on a straight line and

$$|PT2PT3| = ((Z(1)-Z(2))**2)**.5 \qquad (2)$$

This makes PT1PT2PT3 a right triangle, and by the Pythagorean theorem,

$$|PT1PT2|=((X(1)-X2))**2+(Y(1)-Y(2))**2+(Z(1)-Z(2))**2)**.5 \qquad (3)$$

## 6.8 Production Direction

For this purpose we need to define direction angles of a line in space. We begin by letting any line (L) have starting coordinates of X(0), Y(0), Z(0) and ending coordinates of X(1), Y(1), Z(1). Next determine the point distance (D). The direction angles are set as (1) the *x*-direction cosine, (2) the *y*-direction cosine, and (3) the *z*-direction cosine. If we label these angles C1, C2, and C3, respectively, the following equations can be used by the display software:

$$C1 = \frac{X(1)-X(0)}{D}$$

$$C2 = \frac{Y(1)-Y(0)}{D}$$

$$C3 = \frac{Z(1)-Z(0)}{D}$$

If C1, C2, C3 are the direction cosines of a line, then

```
C1**2+C2**2+C3**2 = 1
```

## 6.9 Parametric Production of Lines

In this chapter we use a CDG graphics package designed with parametric equations of lines. There are two systems associated with the parametric equation of a line in space. One is the directed distance just presented and the other is the rectangular coordinate system represented earlier by the ordered triple (x,y,z).

Given a direction line with cosines C1, C2, and C3, let X1, Y1, and Z1 be a point on the line at distance D, then

```
X = X1+C1*D
Y = Y1+C2*D
Z = Z1+C3*D
```

## 6.10 CDG Technical Illustration

CDG is used to define the following:

1. Parts for catalogs (Section 6.11)
2. Solids for visualization (Section 6.12)
3. Point/line/plane relationships (Section 6.13)
4. Point/line/plane analysis (Section 6.14)
5. Developments and Intersections (Section 6.15)

CDG can be used to explain how CADD enables the user to:

1. Display, store, reproduce, modify, or transmit CADD elements of any object involving form so that the output will reveal all the essential facts.
2. Determine from (1) any and all desired facts as to distances, angles, intersections, areas, volumes, and mass properties.
3. Generate from (1) and (2) any constructions required to introduce given distances, angles, intersections, areas, volumes, or mass properties as design data.

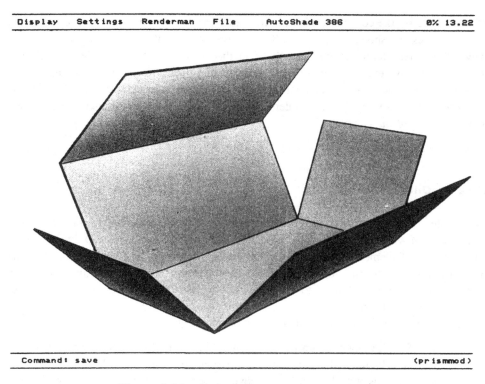

Display    Settings    Renderman    File    AutoShade 386              0% 13.22

Command: save                                                        (prismmod)

**Figure 6.21**  Surface development of a prism.

The purposes of CDG are accomplished through the employment of five CADD principles:

1. Orthographic projection (Figures 6.5 and 6.20)
2. Parallelism (Figures 6.10 and 6.13)
3. Perpendicularity (Figures 6.12 and 6.15)
4. Intersections (Figures 6.14 and 6.17)
5. Developments (Figure 6.21)

## 6.11  Parts Definition

CDG uses the various types of plane surfaces used in descriptive geometry. A plane thus defined can be shown on a VDT by displaying any two lines within the plane surface, as in Figure 6.6. The CADD display screen completely describes the projections of these lines on the coordinate planes. All lines lying in a given plane surface are called coplanar lines, as shown in Figure 6.8. The significant qualities of such lines are that they either intersect or are parallel. Since in theory, every plane in CDG can be extended to infinity, every plane surface displayed may therefore be extended until it intersects at least two of the three coordinate planes. These intersections are called *principal traces*. If two plane surfaces intersect, as in Figure 6.14, they also leave a trace alone the *line of intersection*.

## 6.12   Solid Definition

In Chapter 5 we described the CADD method of solid presentation based on the AutoSolid software approach. This approach allows construction of 3D images from combinations of elementary shapes, such as sphere, cylinder, and toroid. For the purposes of this chapter, the author has added special forms as basic primitives and used Autodesk's polymesh technique to render joined or assembled objects as shown in Figures 6.16, 6.17, and 6.18.

The options available for solid presentation included:

1. Wireform in any axonometric orientation (Figure 6.19), random shaded polygon surfaces (Figure 6.16), or halftone presentations (Figure 6.18)
2. Solid models with hidden-line removal in any axonometric rotation, with color shading in random or halftone patterns (Figure 6.17)
3. Light source for realistic model shades and shadows to include basic primitives for cube, cone, pyramid, sphere, and torus (Figure 6.16)

## 6.13   Point/Line/Plane Relationships

CDG contains the working relationships for constructive geometry: the point, line, and plane combinations that can be displayed in engineering problem solving. Both principal and plane tracing are used throughout the many CADD displays shown as figures in this chapter.

## 6.14   Point/Line/Plane Analysis

CDG also covers the concepts of point/line/plan analysis for:

1. True length of a line (Figure 6.8)
2. Distance from a point to a line (Figure 6.3)
3. Distance between two parallel planes (Figure 6.13)

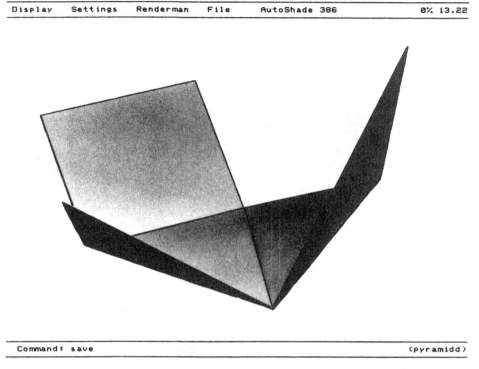

Figure 6.22   Surface development of a pyramid.

4.   True distance between lines
5.   Common perpendiculars (Figures 6.12 and 6.13)

## 6.15   Development and Intersections

CDG can deal with tangent planes and solids, intersection of planes and solids, and development of solids using surfaces, respectively. Each figure cited below presents CADD screen displays showing construction, solution, and analysis of common descriptive geometry problems.

1.   Surface development of a prism (Figure 6.21)
2.   Surface development of a pyramid (Figure 6.22)
3.   Surface development of a cone (Figure 6.23)
4.   Surface development of a cyliner (Figure 6.24)

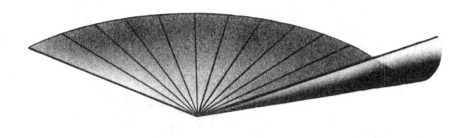

**Figure 6.23**　Surface development of a cone.

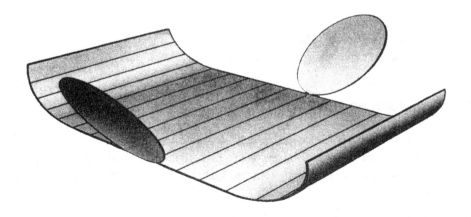

**Figure 6.24**　Surface development of a cylinder.

## Exercises

1.   Select a CADD workstation and sign on the CDG system (the instructions for this will be in the notebook you prepared for the exercises in Chapter 1).
2.   Begin working with the CDG system by building single points in space: two points in the horizontal plane of projection and two related points in the frontal plane. Practice connecting the points to form lines. Connect the lines to form planes, and the planes to form solids.
3.   Display point C as shown below. Consider this point as part of a pictorial object.

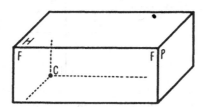

4.   Display point C from above as part of an orthographic projection.

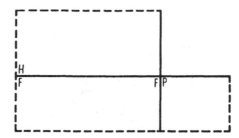

5.   Add a second point to form a line.

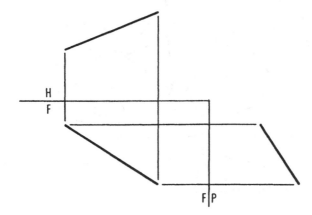

6.  Add a third point to form a plane.

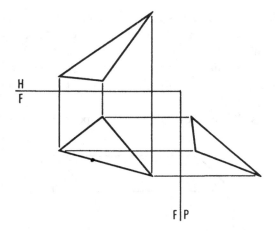

7.  Add additional points to the display to form a solid.

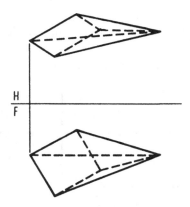

8.  Continue the solid building process with auxiliary views.

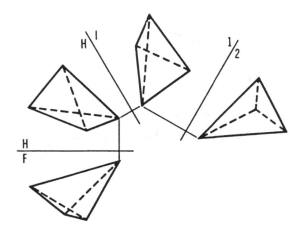

9. Find the true length (TL).

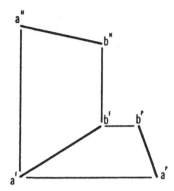

10. Find the slope of the line.

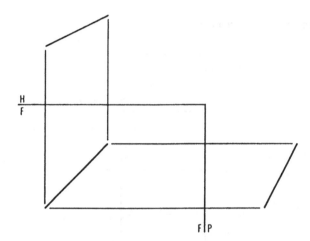

11. Find the bearing of the line.

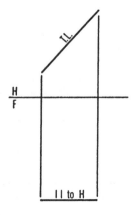

12. Find the intersection of the lines.

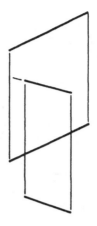

13. Find the parallel lines in a profile view.

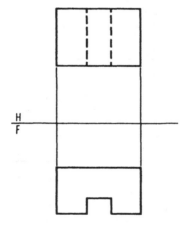

14. Find the point view of the line.

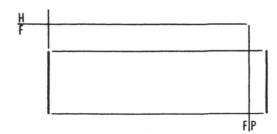

15.   Find the location of the line in the various planes.

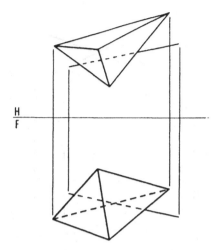

16.   Find the edge view of the plane.

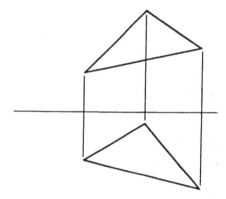

17.   Find the true size of the plane.

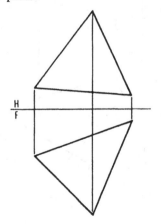

18.  Find the piercing point of the line and plane.

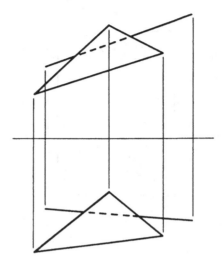

19.  Find the intersection of the planes.

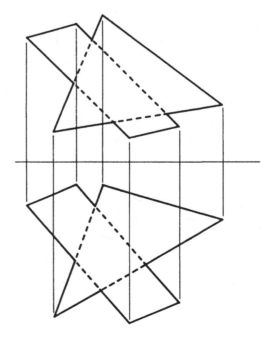

20.  Find the angle between the planes.

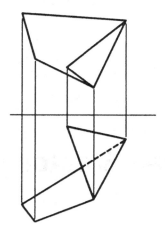

# 7

# Computerized Vector Geometry

Computerized vector geometry (CVG) is the study of graphic statics, with graphics workstation assistance. The application of graphic statics to the solution of structural problems has been in wide use by engineers and architects for many years. The addition of the graphics workstation used in Chapter 6, called CVG, is fairly new. Like CDG, it contains powerful tools for problem solution. CVG representation of the forces that act in various members of a structural framework possess many advantages over manual solution; the primary advantage, beyond presenting a graphical picture of the stresses, is that most problems can be solved with the speed and accuracy of the computer.

With the CDG skills outlined in Chapter 6, stresses may be obtained much more accurately than the various members can be sized, since in sizing we must select, from a handbook, members capable of withstanding loads equal to or greater than the design load. Using CVG, the designer computes a size and then applies a factor of safety when designing any structure.

Customarily, problems in statics are solved by either graphical or algebraic methods. In this chapter the author has assumed that the reader is familiar with one or the other. With no previous background in statics, the reader will gain little from the study of how to automate it. Before proceeding further, review the common terms of graphic statics shown in Table 7.1. Many excellent references exist for studying the terminology listed. The reader should consult a reference source if any of the terms are unclear. We begin the study of CVG by building directly on the skills learned in Chapter 6.

**Table 7.1** Common Terms of Graphic Statics

| | | |
|---|---|---|
| Statics | Force | Elements of force |
| Vector | Tension | Compression |
| Shear | Equilibrium | Equilibrant |
| Magnitude scale | Structural scale | Coplanar |
| Noncoplanar | Concurrent | Nonconcurrent |
| Resultant of a force | Moment of a force | Couples |
| Funicular polygon | Space diagram | Stress diagram |
| Load line | Reactions | Free-body diagram |

## 7.1 Vector Notation

In Chapter 6, line segments were labelled "starting point" and "ending point" because they were not vectors. They were known as *scalar values*. In this chapter we deal with line segments known as *vectors*. This is the name applied to a line of scaled length that represents the magnitude and direction of a force. An arrowhead placed on the line, shows the *sense* (which way the force acts). The next noticeable difference is that vectors use *Bow's notation* for labeling. In example (1), CDG notation looks as follows:

$$Ah \underline{\hspace{3cm}} Bh \tag{1}$$

whereas CVG notation using Bow's labeling looks as follows:

$$
\begin{array}{c}
A \\
\longrightarrow \\
B
\end{array}
\tag{2}
$$

You will note that the space around the vector has been labeled. Both are referenced AB, (1) representing a horizontal projection of a line segment. Vector notation should not be confused with Bow's notation. Bow's notation is the labeling of a diagram to read around two or more vectors called *joints* (2). The reading is made in a clockwise direction for convenience.

In example (2), the vector needs additional notation to indicate the type of vector. If it is coplanar, its magnitude can be labeled. We can check for this by using another VPORT, as shown in Chapter 6 and example (3).

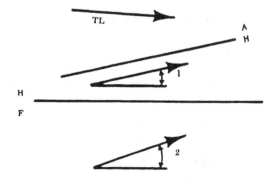

$$\tag{3}$$

This vector may be described as follows:

AB  =  TL⌊θ1,θ2                                                          (4)

Here vector notation is used to say the following: a vector AB is TL vector units long (magnitude) and the angles from the planar references are 1 and 2 units long.

## 7.2  Vector Addition and Subtraction

Figure 7.1 illustrates three joints, AB, CD, and EF. We use these three joints to demonstrate vector addition, shown in Figure 7.2, and vector subtraction, shown in Figure 7.3. The parallelogram method of adding vectors A-B and C-D is used in Figure 7.2. In this case the vector sum of A and B (called a *resultant*) is the diagonal of the parallelogram emanating from the origin point shown in Figure 7.1.

Figure 7.3 shows the parallelogram method for subtracting vector B from A and F from E. The vectors to be subtracted is reversed in direction and then added to the other vector. In this case the result is called the *equilibrant* of the joint.

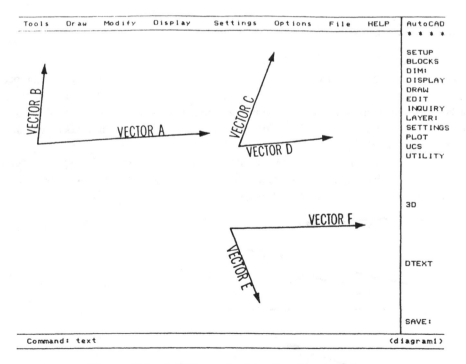

**Figure 7.1**   Addition and subtraction demonstration.

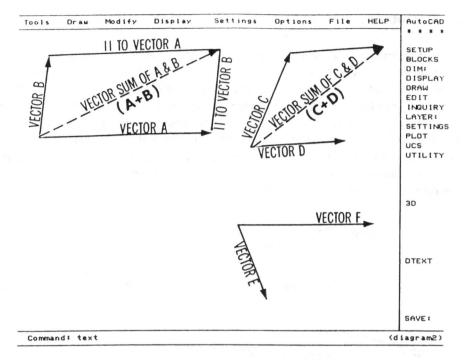

**Figure 7.2**   Addition of A-B and C-D.

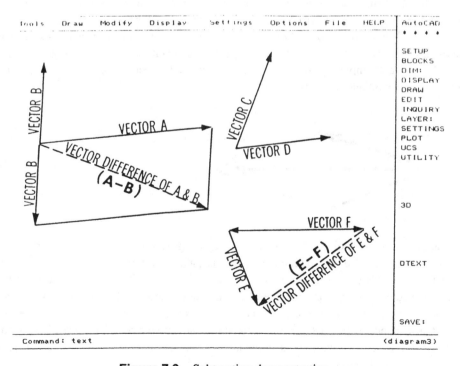

**Figure 7.3**   Subtraction demonstration.

## 7.3  Resultants

If a group of vectors describing a system (joints) are in equilibrium, the system is said to be *balanced*. The resultant of this system is always zero. Systems are either balanced or unbalanced. Vectors represent abstract quantities of the physical system. Two or more vectors acting together are required to describe a system. To solve a problem in which vectors are used, a resultant is often found. It is found by the use of two diagrams. One, the *space diagram,* shows the relationship in the physical system and indicates how the vectors are applied. The second, the *stress diagram,* is built from the space diagram to determine characteristics of the system (i.e., balanced or unbalanced).

Suppose that we look at a simple example:

(5)

If the two vectors act simultaneously at point A, the result will be a path, shown dashed below.

(6)

The resultant, then, is the result of two or more vectors acting on a system at the same time. If the vectors act independently, the path taken will be A to C to B along the vector lines. When only two vectors are contained in the system, a principle of the parallelogram of forces is employed in finding the resultant of two vectors acting on a body. By using example (7), the body would be moved directly along the diagonal connection of the parallelogram (R).

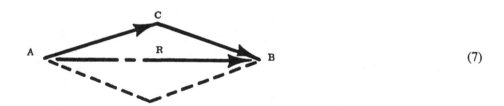

(7)

Suppose that we look at the system shown in Figure 7.4. If the two vectors act simultaneously at point 0, the addition will be the path shown in Figure 7.5. The resultant of the system is shown in Figure 7.6. Remember, the resultant is the addition of two or more vectors acting on a system at the same time. This system is *oblique* (noncoplanar) with two view ports (H and F), as demonstrated in Chapter 6. If the vectors act in a noncoplanar fashion, the resultant is the true length of the addition in both views. If the system of vectors is coplanar, as shown in Figure 7.7, the addition of vectors is the final resultant.

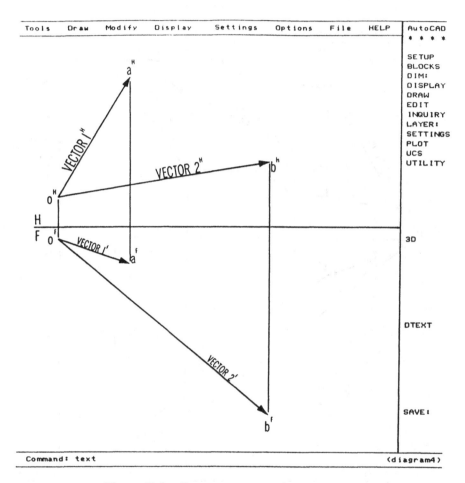

**Figure 7.4**   Concurrent, noncoplanar vectors.

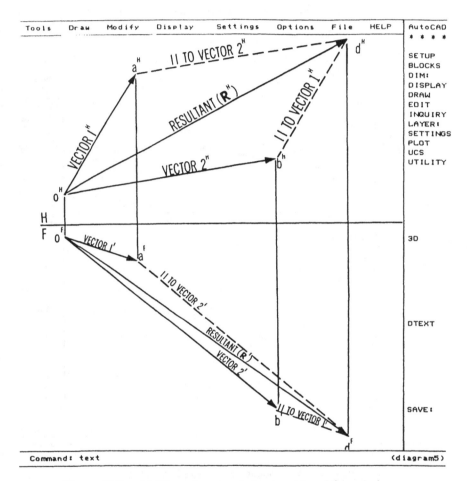

**Figure 7.5**   Addition of vectors in horizontal and frontal views.

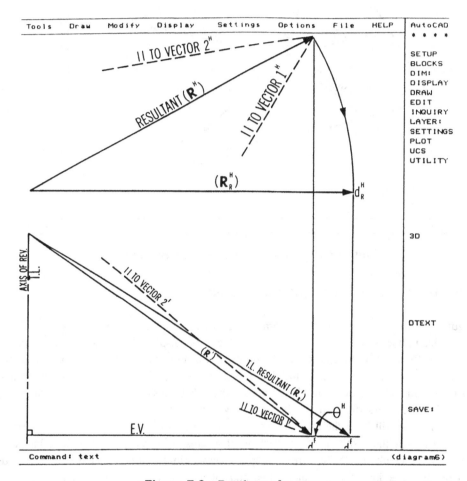

**Figure 7.6**  Resultant of system.

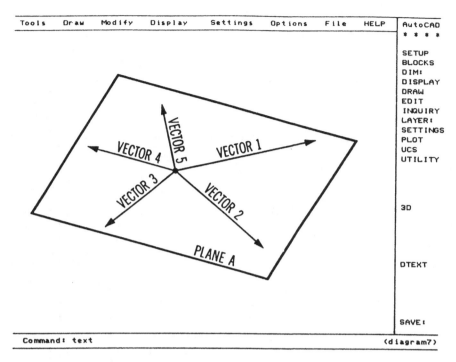

**Figure 7.7**   Concurrent, coplanar system of vectors.

## 7.4   Resultant of a Coplanar System

Figure 7.8 illustrates a space diagram for a system of concurrent coplanar forces of given magnitude and directions. This system can be displayed as a stress diagram, as shown in Figure 7.9. In this diagram we begin with the first vector, $F_1$, from the space diagram and connect $F_2$ to it at the determined angle of 60°. Each vector is connected, tip to tail, in this fashion until all five vectors have been displayed as the stress diagram.

After the stress diagram has been displayed we may want to find the single force (resultant) that will have the same effect as the five vectors. Figure 7.10 closes the stress diagram and is the resultant of the system. If a stress diagram is closed, it is balanced and has no resultant. If the stress diagram shown in Figure 7.9 is to be balanced, change the direction of the resultant line and label it the equilibrant in Figure 7.10.

## 7.5   Noncoplanar Resultants

All noncoplanar systems require two view ports to find the resultant. In Figure 7.11 three vectors are displayed in two view ports. Either a stress diagram in both view ports is required or space volumes may be used. Figure 7.12 shows the addition of parallelograms to form the space volume. Figure 7.13 illustrates the ease of resultant (oblique lengths) in the horizontal and frontal view ports. To determine the magnitude of the resultant, find the true length of the resultant by rotation as shown in Figure 7.6.

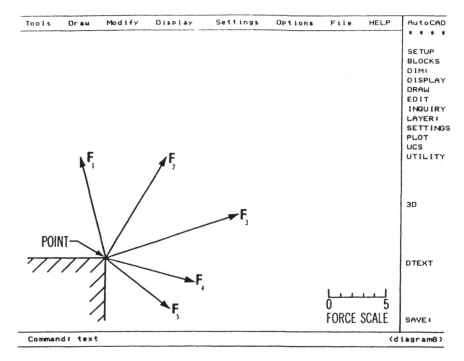

**Figure 7.8** Space diagram for forces of given magnitude and direction.

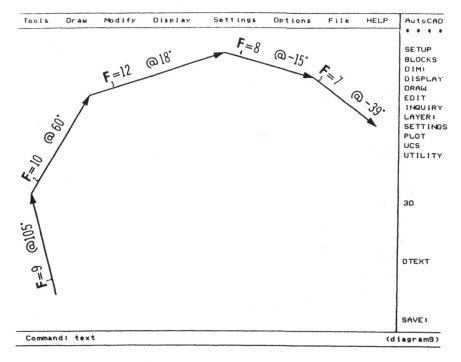

**Figure 7.9** Stress diagram for forces of given magnitude and direction.

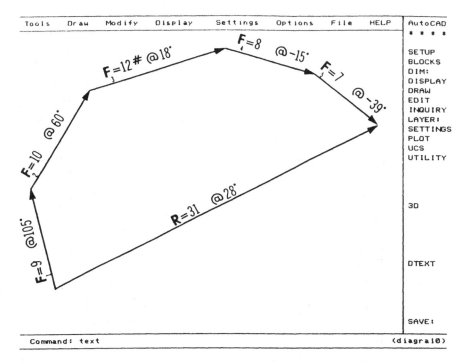

**Figure 7.10**    Resultant for forces of given magnitude and direction.

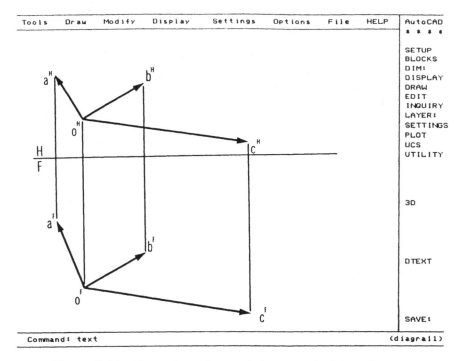

**Figure 7.11**    Noncoplanar forces of given magnitude and direction.

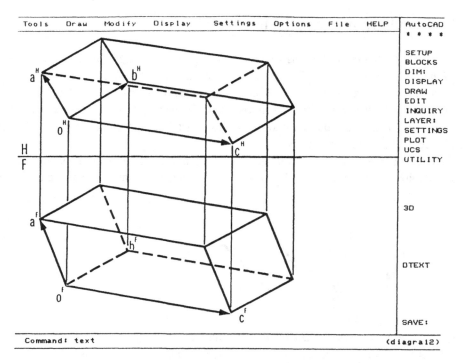

**Figure 7.12**   Space volume for forces of given magnitude and direction.

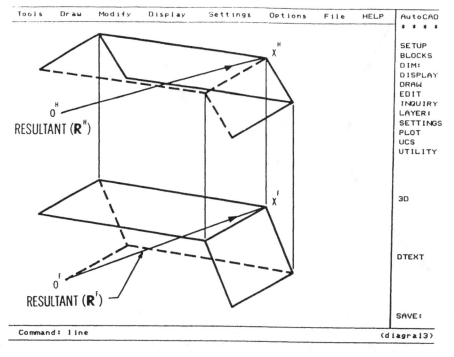

**Figure 7.13**   Resultant for noncoplanar forces.

## 7.6   Resultant and Application Point

The general term for the process of replacing a group of vectors by a single vector is *combination* or *composition*. This process is the addition of two or more vectors. The opposite process, that of replacing a single vector by two or more vectors having the same effect, is called *resolution*. Each vector in the new system is called a *component* of the given vector. Resolution and composition are useful techniques when studying nonconcurrent systems of vectors.

Nonconcurrent coplanar forces may be combined to show a point of application. The combination or addition will illustrate a common resultant. Let us begin with an example (8).

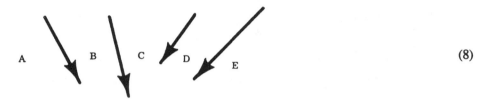

                                                                                    (8)

Here four vectors are separated by Bow's notation: A, B, C, D, and E. They are not concurrent, and they do not act parallel, but they are coplanar. A stress diagram is laid out beside the space diagram as in example (9).

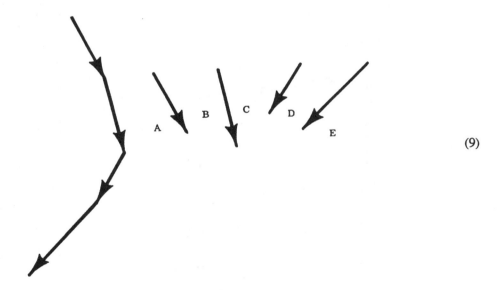

                                                                                    (9)

This shows clearly that a resultant is present. The magnitude of the resultant can be displayed, but the point of application has not been located. In example (10), a convenient point beside the stress diagram is constructed. This point is called a *pole point*. From the pole point, lay out construction lines to each tip and tail.

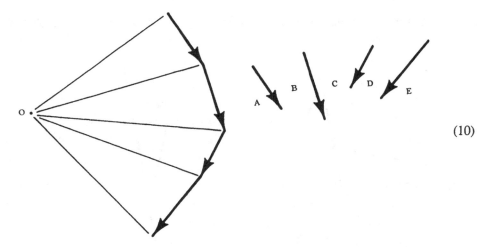

(10)

The next step is to label the work done in example (10); this is shown in example (11).

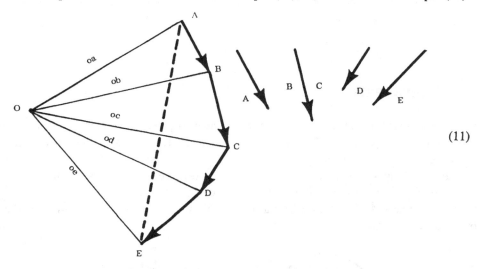

(11)

The last steps in the location of the point of application would be the construction of the funicular polygon, as in example (12).

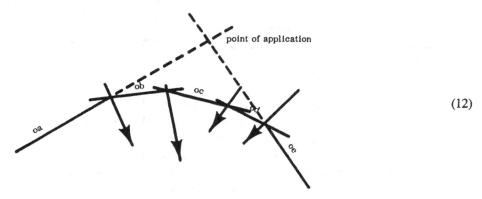

(12)

Transfer (COPY) the resultant through the point of application as shown in example (13).

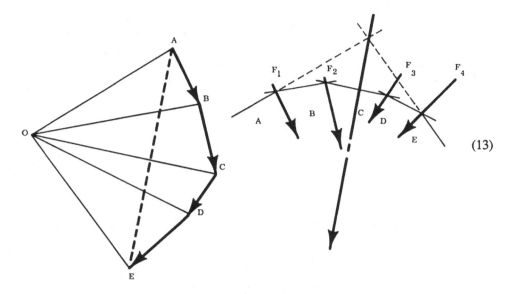

(13)

## 7.7    Equilibrants

If a single vector is added to an unbalanced system to produce equilibrium, that vector is known as an *equilibrant*. The equilibrant in an unbalanced system will always have the same location and magnitude as the resultant of that system but will have the opposite sense. Many statics problems can be worked because an equilibrant can be added to a system or the system is already in a state of equilibrium.

In example (14), let us assume that the wheel in the space diagram is to be pushed over the 6-inch block:

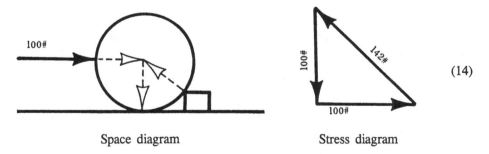

(14)

Space diagram                                    Stress diagram

The horizontal force tending to push the wheel is applied level with the centerline of the wheel. A stress diagram of the concurrent system can be displayed on the VDT because we know that the system is in equilibrium. The stress diagram indicates the direction and magnitude of the forces in the balanced system. As shown in the space diagram, the lines of action of the three forces meet in a common point (concurrency), and the stress diagram closes (equilibrium). A slight increase in horizontal force will produce motion.

The next question that might be asked is whether or not the centerline is the most ideal place to apply a pushing force if labor saving is important. Two other points of application are selected in example (15).

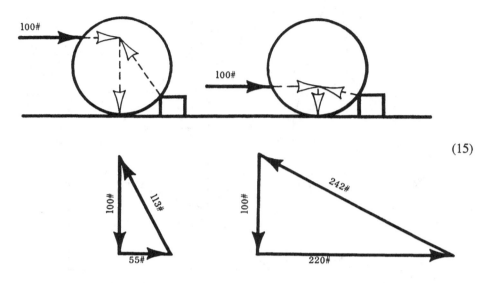

(15)

## 7.8 Space Diagrams

The use of simple diagrams in space has been illustrated throughout this chapter. The bulk of CVG problems fall into the noncoplanar category. Figure 7.14 is an example of this category; compare it with Figure 7.7. Bow's notation comes in handy in labeling more than one view of a single system of vectors. Example (16) illustrates the concurrent, noncoplanar system.

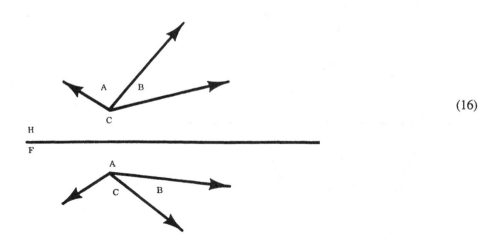

(16)

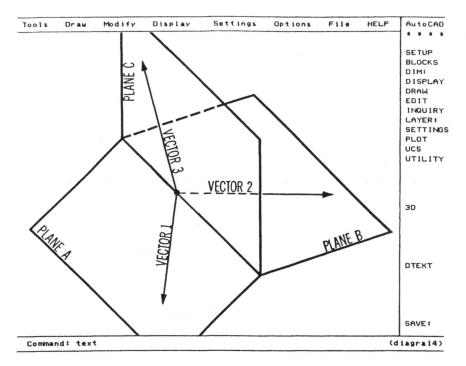

**Figure 7.14**   Noncoplanar system of vectors.

By this method, letters or numbers are placed on both sides of each vector shown in the space diagram. In example (17), nonconcurrent, noncoplanar vectors are displayed.

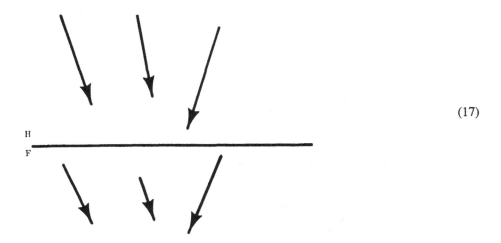

(17)

## 7.9  Stress Diagrams

The vector or stress diagram is displayed for determining certain characteristics of the system. The stress diagram represents the magnitudes and directions of the forces called for in the space diagram. Example (18) illustrates both the space and stress diagram for the same system of vectors.

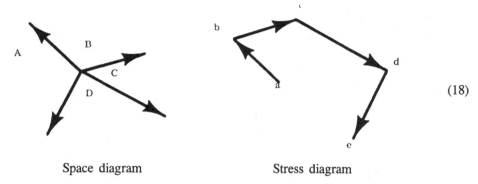

               (18)

Space diagram            Stress diagram

Nonconcurrent, coplanar systems may use three types of diagrams, as in example (19).

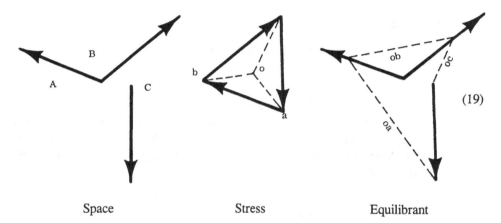

               (19)

Space           Stress           Equilibrant

## 7.10  Simple Structure Analysis

When CVG is used to design a simple truss, computer displays are used to determine stresses in the various members of the truss. Any structure must be designed to carry its own weight in addition to the weights or loads specified. For convenience in this section, we shall assume that the weight of the truss is included with the given loading. The weights of roofing members can also be determined by the following:

```
Steel:  W = 1/2AL(1+1/101)
Wood:   W = 3/4AL(1+1/101)
```

where L = span in feet
     A = distance in feet between adjacent trusses
     W = weight of a single truss

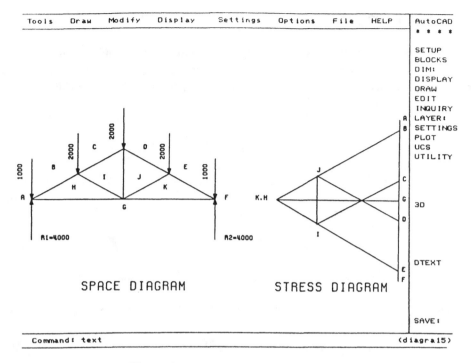

**Figure 7.15** Truss design and analysis.

Figure 7.15 shows a typical solution when determining stresses in the members of a truss. The truss is anchored at both ends and is subjected to dead loads concentrated at points where the truss members frame (connect) together. When analyzing stresses by CVG, the space diagram is displayed first, Bow's notation is applied, and the stress diagram is written as follows:

1. Start by displaying the load line and dividing it proportionately between the reactions at both fixed ends.
2. The load line is vertical, since the loads act vertically. The length of the load line represents the sum of the loads when displayed to scale.
3. The loads in this example are symmetrical, the reactions R1 and R2 are equal, or 4000.
4. The first line in the stress diagram should be displayed horizontally through point G and toward the left edge of the screen so it cuts vector BH displayed through B on the load line and is parallel to truss member BH in the space diagram.
5. All vectors in the stress diagram should be labeled.
6. Each joint in the space diagram, from left to right, must be matched by a closed polygon in the stress diagram. The completed stress diagram is a series of closed polygons (equilibrium diagrams).

7. Each vector in the stress diagram is parallel to the corresponding member in the space diagram. While each vector in the stress diagram is automatically at the same scale as used to plot the load line, individual member stresses can be calculated and displayed for our use.

## Exercises

1. Find the resultant of the concurrent, coplanar systems of vectors.

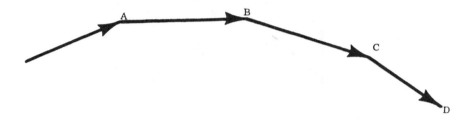

2. Display the stress diagram for the space diagram.

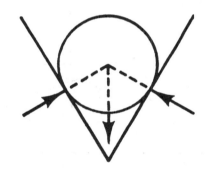

3. Create the vector diagram for the jib crane supporting a 2-ton weight.

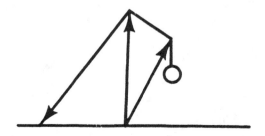

4.   Construct a stress diagram for the support frame with a 1-ton weight.

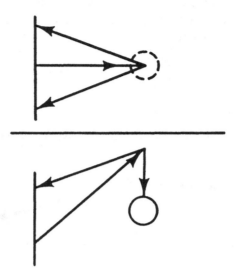

5.   Calculate the amount of the resultant if the display scale is known.

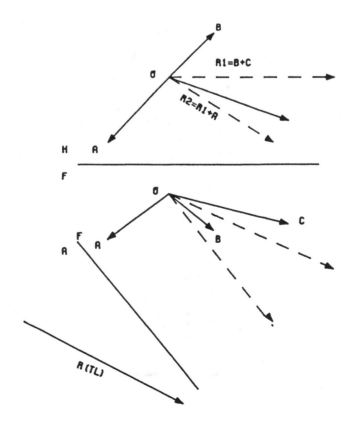

6. What is the value of the equilibrant in the noncoplanar system?

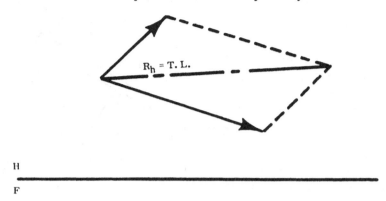

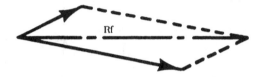

7. Calculate the value of the resultant in this system.

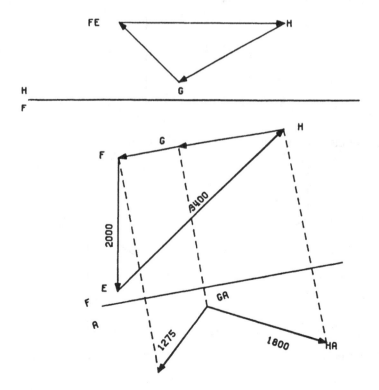

8.  What is the stress in members A and B?

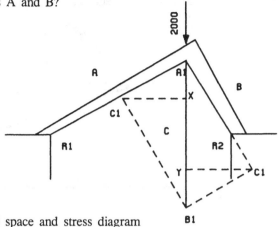

Combined space and stress diagram

9.  Display the equilibrant diagram.

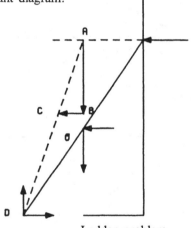

Ladder problem

10. Calculate the reactions right and left on this truss.

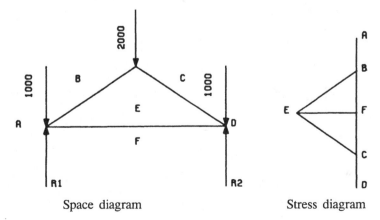

Space diagram                           Stress diagram

# 8

# Computerized Solid Geometry

Computerized solid geometry (CSG) is the study of computer-generated modeling, with Autodesk's AME (Advanced Modeling Extension) assistance. Like CDG and CVG, CSG contains powerful tools for simple model construction. In this chapter we take you through a series of steps that will enable you to create a CSG model using AME. AME creates models using a set of built-in primitives. Boolean operations such as union, difference, and intersection let you modify the primitives to define the shape of your desired model.

To create a solid model you have to load AME if it is not part of your current Autodesk release. This is done on releases prior to 12 by selecting the `OPTIONS` pulldown menu. Move the cursor to the `SOLID` and select `load.AME`. You now see the `SOLID` menu opened revealing one of its submenus, `sol-Prism`. The other submenus of SOLID are listed at the bottom of the other pull-down menus. Any of these may be selected directly to work the many examples throughout this chapter.

## 8.1  Solid Model Classification

Use Table 8.1 to review the CADD classification of solid composition. Solids are divided into two groups, wireform and geometric. Wireforms are either single (cylinders and cones) or warped. Warped solids can be displayed from the following databases:

1. Hyperbolic paraboloid
2. Hyperboloid of revolution
3. Helicoid
4. Conoid
5. General directices

Geometric solids are considered to be a sphere, ellipsoid, paraboloid, hyperboloid, or torus. Geometric solids can be displayed from the following databases:

1. Sweeps
2. Two-axis equal
3. General
4. Three-axis unequal
5. Elliptical

**Table 8.1** Classification of Models

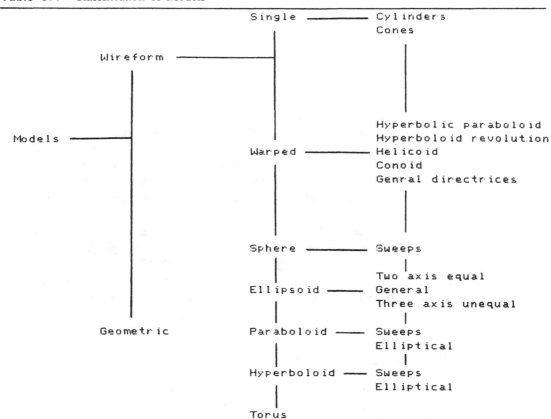

## 8.2 Presentation of Models

At the start of your modeling session you must set the viewing space to accommodate the dimensions of the object. CTRL-C may be used in case of an error in executing a command during this process. All text that appears at the command line within angle brackets (< >) are default settings of AME. The default settings of the viewing space are lower left corner (0.000,0.000) and upper right corner (12.000,9.000). Begin this process by

```
Command: limits
ON/OFF/<lower left corner><0.000,0.000>:-5,-5
Upper right corner <12.000,9.000>: 30,20
```

You may select a grid spacing of 0.25 unit to aid in constructing the model by

```
Command: grid
Grid spacing(x) or ON/OFF/Snap/Aspect <0.000>:0.25
```

Set the snap to 0.25, and to ensure that you have access to the entire viewing space, zoom into the viewing space by

```
Command: zoom
All/Center/Dynamic/Extents/Left/Previous/Vmax/Window/<A>:
```

**Figure 8.1** Grid background for CSG model.

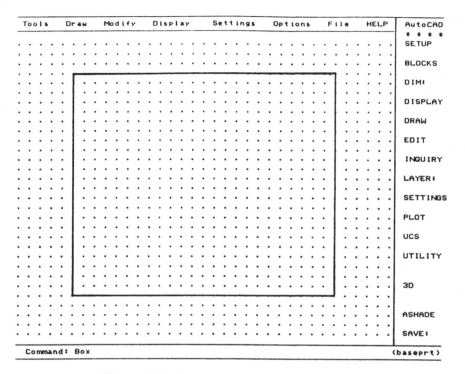

**Figure 8.2**   Sol-Prisms menu selection of box.

## 8.3  Prisms

As you begin the creation of a CSG model the workstation screen looks like Figure 8.1. The direction of the viewing space is given as (0,0,1), that is, along the Z axis. Your vantage point for viewing the model is like a top view. Begin the model by selecting Box from the Sol-Prism pull-down menu. The position of this prism is LLC (0,0) and URC (24,16) and using

```
Corner of box: 0,0
Cube/Length/<Other corner>: 24,24
Height: 4
```

The display screen looks like Figure 8.2 with a top view of a 6-inch-square prism. If your display does not look like Figure 8.2, stop and set the scale so that the image at your workstation is similar. This will make it possible to create a complete CSG model by following the text and figures of this chapter.

## 8.4 Open Cylinders

Holes may be placed in the prism by using cylinder from the Sol-Prism pull-down menu. Position the first hole as shown in Figure 8.3, assuming center points of the cylinders as shown and a radius of 1 grid unit.

```
Elliptical/<center point>: 3,3
Diameter/<radius>: 1
Height of cylinder: 4
```

The remaining cylinders can be displayed by copying the first one to the required locations, as shown in Figure 8.3.

```
Command: copy
Select objects:
```

Remember that you copy objects by placing the screen cursor box around the object to be copied. It should be highlighted now and you can move and copy the three additional cylinders. These cylinders are not holes until they are subtracted from the prism. From the options in Sol-Prism select Modify and a new menu, Sol-Modify appears. Select Subtract from the menu as

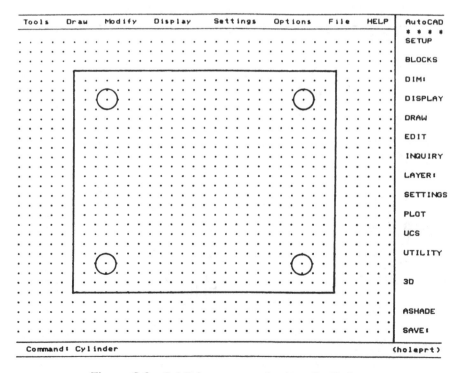

**Figure 8.3** Sol-Prisms menu selection of cylinder.

```
Source objects ...
Select objects:
```

The source objects are the objects from which you want to subtract other primitives (base prism). Position the cursor on one of the sides of the base prism and select it and then

```
Select objects: return
Objects to subtract from them ...
Select objects:
```

Select all four cylinders to indicate that they are to be subtracted (holes).

## 8.5   Viewing the Progress

At this point in the CSG model building we are unable to see the entire model (base with four holes). To view it from a different vantage point, turn off the grid and type

```
Command: vpoint
Rotate/<0.000,0.000,1.000>: 1,1,1
```

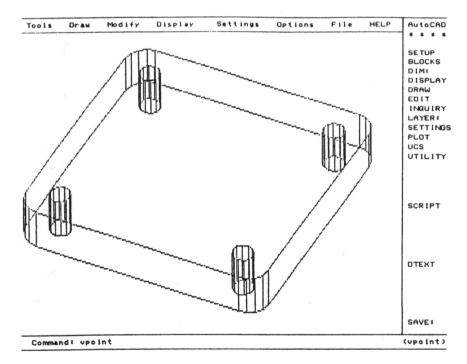

**Figure 8.4**   Model displayed in new VPOINT.

From the `Sol-Modify` menu select `Fillet` as

```
Select edges to be filleted:
```
Position the cursor on each of the four vertical edges of the base and enter each. These should now be highlighted:

```
Diameter/<radius> of fillet <0.000>: 3
```

will create a display as shown in Figure 8.4. To return to model construction:

```
Command: vpoint:
Rotate/<1.000,1.000,1.000>: 0,0,1
```

## 8.6 Closed Cylinders

All the AME primitives displayed so far have their bases at the base level (elevation is 0). The height of the base is 4 units. To place a closed or solid cylinder on the top surface of the base, we will need to change the elevation of the placement cylinder by

```
Command: elev
New current elevation <0.000>: 4
New current thickness <0.000>: 0
```

From the `Sol-Prism` menu select `Cylinder` and place it as shown in Figure 8.5. The next step is to integrate the two parts (base prism and closed cylinder) into one object. From `Sol-Prism` select `Modify`, then select `Union` from the `Modify` menu as

```
Select objects:
```

First select the lower base prism, then select the top closed cylinder. You now have a single object.

At this point we can continue with the UNION of cylinders as shown in Figure 8.6, which has displayed as an open cylinder subtracted from the solid closed cylinder, and Figure 8.7, which is the addition of another solid closed cylinder with a new elevation. This process is easy to continue; suppose that we change elevations again and add an array of smaller cylinders as shown in Figure 8.8.

This is done by using a ZOOM window as shown in Figure 8.9. Now that we have enlarged this portion of the CSG model, we can make six copies of the smaller cylinders in the form of a circular array by

```
Command: array
Select objects: last
1 found
Select objects:
Rect or Polar array: P
Center point of array:
Number of items: 6
Angle to fill <360>:
Rotate objects <Y>: N
```

Your screen should now look like Figure 8.10.

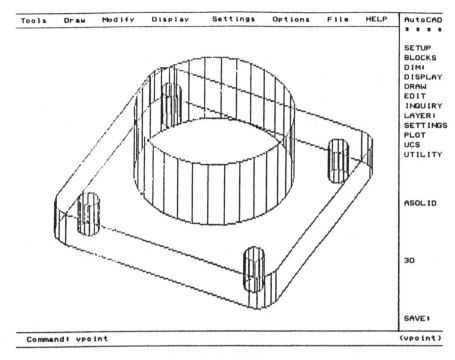

**Figure 8.5**  Model displayed with closed cylinder UNION.

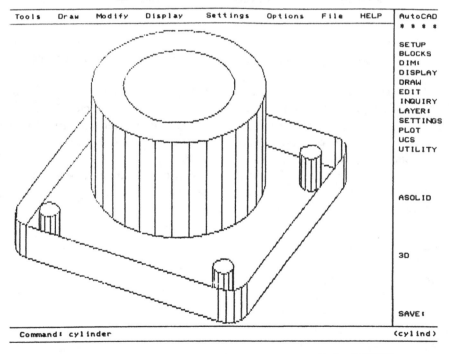

**Figure 8.6**  Model displayed with closed/open cylinder UNION.

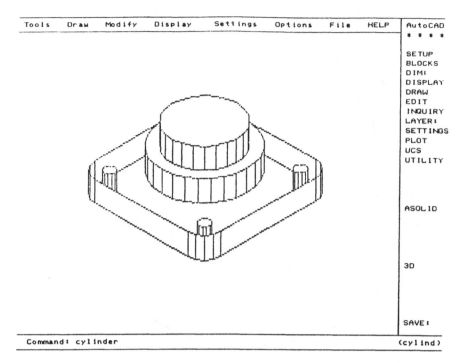

**Figure 8.7** Model displayed with closed/closed cylinder UNION.

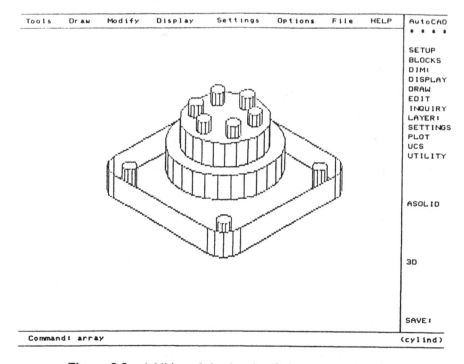

**Figure 8.8** Addition of six closed cylinders at new elevation.

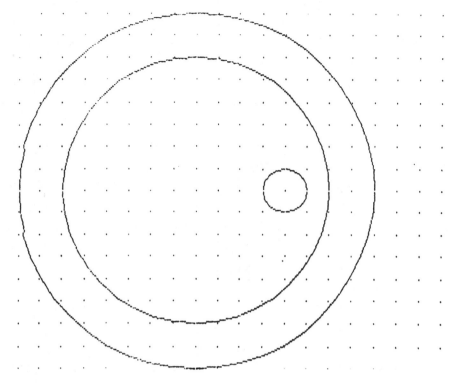

**Figure 8.9**   Screen image after ZOOM command.

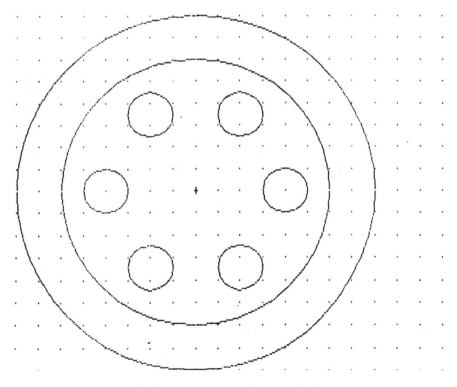

**Figure 8.10**   Screen image after ARRAY command.

## 8.7 Wireform Models

The CSG model created in Sections 8.3 to 8.6 was limited to prisms and cylinders. You may want to try other combinations of primitives by selecting an exercise at the end of the chapter. All of the models that are created in this fashion are called *wireforms*. By using the command HIDE, as was done in Figures 8.6 to 8.8, some of the transparent viewing is clipped for better viewing, but these are not CSG models yet. To view the wireform as a solid body, it is required to transform the model into a meshed body. You can do this by using Sol-Modify and selecting DISPLAY. A new menu appears as Sol-Display. Select Mesh from this menu as

```
Select solids to be meshed
Select objects:
Select objects:
```

## 8.8 Geometric Models

Geometric models are not restricted to primitive building blocks. For example, suppose that we wished to create the model shown in Figure 8.11. This requires more than

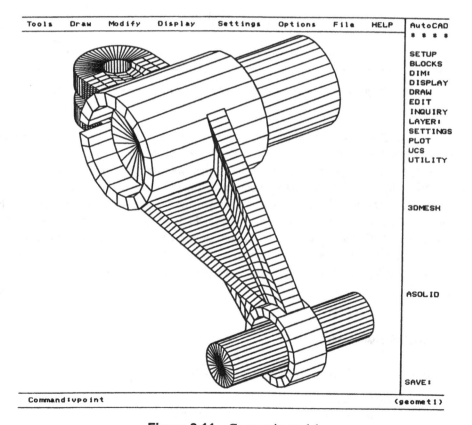

**Figure 8.11** Geometric model.

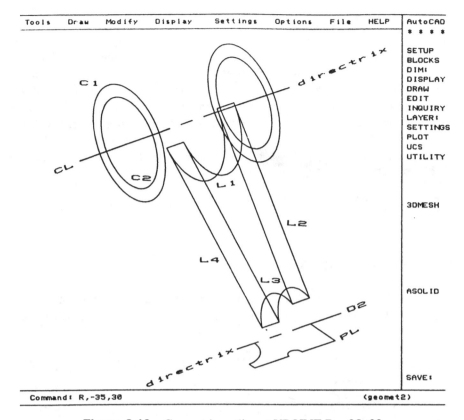

**Figure 8.12**   Geometric outline at VPOINT R, –35, 30.

simple boolean elements. Beginning at the top of the model, it is a hollow cylinder connected to a tapered prism connected to three different-sized hollow cylinders. The AME primitive approach is not the answer. Suppose that we begin the design of this model by indicating the limits of the surface boundaries for the three main elements as shown in Figure 8.12. The top, hollow cylinder is shown by two sets of concentric circles. In Figure 8.12 they appear as viewed through VPOINT:R,–35,30. Next, the tapered prism is outlined to UNION with the top and bottom cylinder sets. Finally, only the directrix and the profile line are given for the bottom cylinders. Whenever general directrices are given, as in the top and bottom cylinders, sweep may be used to create the model element.

## 8.9  Model Sweeps

We begin the geometric model example by sweeping the top pair of cylinders as

```
Command: tabsurf
Select path curve: (see C1 in Figure 8.12)
```

```
Select directrix: (see CL in Figure 8.12)
```

Repeat this process for C2 using the same directrix. Now move down to the second directrix, labeled D2, and select the following:

```
Command: revsurf
Select path curve: (see PL in Figure 8.12)
Select axis rotation: (see D2 directrix)
Start angle <0>: 0
Included angle <360>: 360
```

## 8.10 Two-Axis Models

We are building a two-axis model as outlined in Figure 8.12. To complete the model as shown in Figure 8.13, we will need to create surfaces between the sweeps as

```
Command: rulesurf
Select first defining curve: (use C1)
Select second defining curve: (use C2)
```

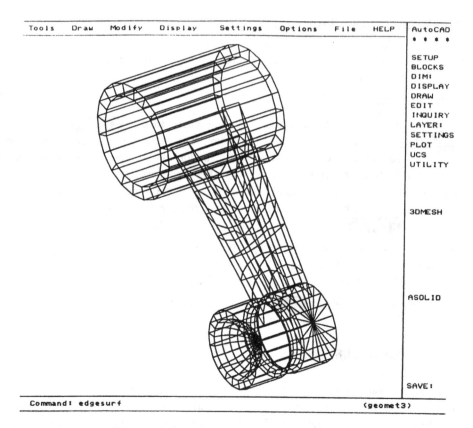

**Figure 8.13**  Wireform of geometric model.

We are now ready to move to the tapered prism.

```
Command: setvar
Variable name <surftab1>:
New value for surftab1 <20>: 8
```

This will increase the size of the mesh for the prism.

```
Command: rulesurf
Select first defining curve: (use L1)
Select second defining curve: (use L2)
```

Repeat the process for L3 and L4.

```
Command: edgesurf
Select edge 1: (use L1)
Select edge 2: (use C1)
Select edge 3: (use L3)
Select edge 4: (use PL)
```

Repeat the process for the back of the tapered prism and Figure 8.13 is now complete.

## 8.11  Hidden-Line Removal

The geometric model is fully meshed and can be viewed with hidden lines removed as seen in Figure 8.14 by

```
Command: hide
```

To view the model as a shaded body, move the cursor to the DISPLAY menu. Select the Shade option from the bottom of the menu. The options for further input appear in the side scroll menu area. The shade if option allows you to set the degree of shadow for the 3D shaded model. Values range between 1 and 100. The shade edge option allows you to view the shaded model without the edges highlighted (256-col), with the edges highlighted (256-edg), only as a regular 3D shaded solid with edges filled. Select Shadeif and respond:

```
New value for SHADEIF<70>: 90
Select the SHADE EDGE:
Select the 256-col option:
```

You are now ready to select SHADE from the top of the menu.

## 8.12  Model Modifications

Several model modifications are shown in Figure 8.15. Beginning at the top, two half cylinder/prisms with a hole were added to the top hollow cylinder. A closed cylinder was inserted into the top hollow cylinder. At the bottom the three-part cylinder produced

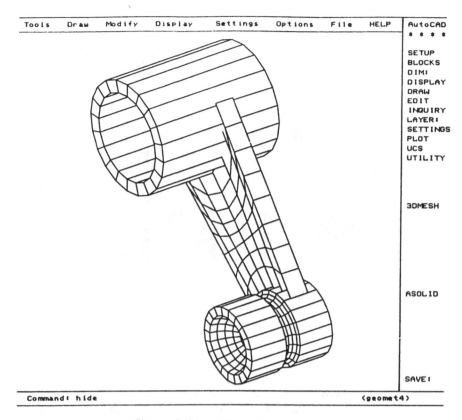

Tools   Draw   Modify   Display   Settings   Options   File   HELP   AutoCAD
* * * *

SETUP
BLOCKS
DIM:
DISPLAY
DRAW
EDIT
INQUIRY
LAYER:
SETTINGS
PLOT
UCS
UTILITY

3DMESH

ASOLID

SAVE:

Command: hide                                                    (geomet4)

**Figure 8.14**   Hidden-line removal.

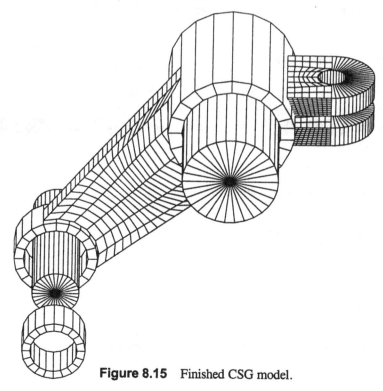

**Figure 8.15**   Finished CSG model.

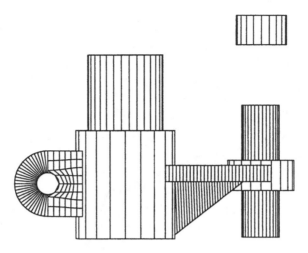

**Figure 8.16**   View selection.

by a single sweep has been replaced by a single hollow cylinder, an open cylinder has been prepared to be inserted into the bottom cylinder, and a closed cylinder will be placed inside the open cylinder. Once the modifications have been done, new viewing positions may be examined as shown in Figure 8.16.

## 8.13   Model Properties

AME can calculate the values of certain properties of the model, such as mass, center of gravity, volume, and moment of inertia, based on the default material taken as mild steel. Locate the `Sol-modify` menu item and select `INQUIRY`. Find `MassPropert` from INQUIRY and respond

```
Select objects:
```

Select any surface of the model with your cursor.

```
Select objects:
Write to a file <Y>:
save
quit
```

## Exercises

Create CSG models for each numbered part of the following diagrams.

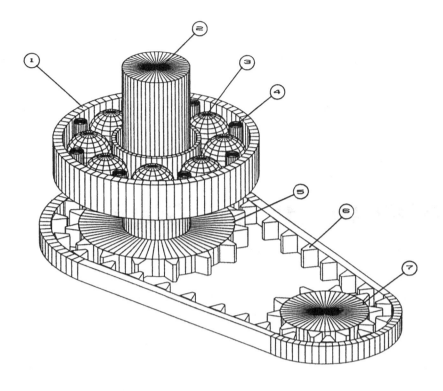

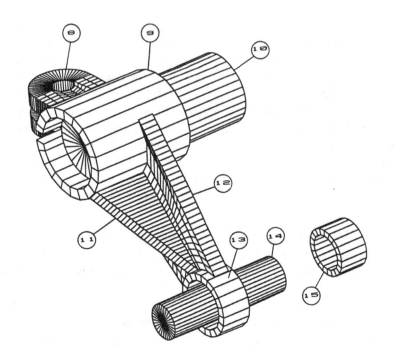

# 9

# CADD Charts and Graphs

The use of CADD to produce charts or graphs systematically during the design process has been well documented by a number of industrial organizations. The most common industrial documentation has been a collection of software routines such as SAS or the Tektronix Advanced Graphics Package. Either charts of graphs can be produced.

*Webster's Dictionary* defines a *chart* as "a sheet showing facts graphically or in tabular form or as a graph showing changes in temperature, variation in population, or prices." A *graph* is defined as "a diagram representing the relationship between two or more factors by means of a series of connected points or by bars, curves, or lines." It is obvious that the editors of the dictionary regard the two terms as synonymous. Most recent computer graphics texts do not distinguish between the two. The present author, however, believes that the two terms should be distinguished for engineering applications and as defines them as follows:

Chart: a more-or-less pictorial computer graphics presentation of facts. It should be pointed out that facts presented by charts are easy to read and quite meaningful to the layperson. Therefore, charts are seen in newspapers, magazines, and the like.

Graph: a presentation of data plotted in one of the many formats where each point is connected with the following adjacent point by a line. There may be more than one set of data per sheet. Graphs are used by engineers to illustrate

trends, to predict, to develop an equation for a certain behavior, to present results of test data obtained in experiments, and to correlate the observations of
natural phenomena.

## 9.1 Analysis of Design Data

Before a proposed design is accepted, it must be subjected to a careful analysis. During
this process the computer data provided must be evaluated and interpreted by the engineer. Most frequently, data are submitted in numerical form, and interpretation is often
a lengthy and difficult procedure. Thus to ensure that the engineer and each member of
the design team understands all aspects of the project, it is convenient to convert numerical computer data to a more customary form that will permit ready understanding.

Before selecting the type of chart or graph to illustrate the design data, consideration
must be given to its use. If it is to be used to determine numerical values or reading
numbers, it would be a *quantitative* chart or graph. If it is used to present comparative
relationships, it is called *qualitative*. Since there are many ways available to present data,
the purpose must be established before the graph or chart is created.

## 9.2 Creating a Basic Graph

To create a simple graph as shown in Figure 9.1, it is necessary to prepare the data that
are to be shown on the VDT. Two data lists will be necessary: one for the horizontal

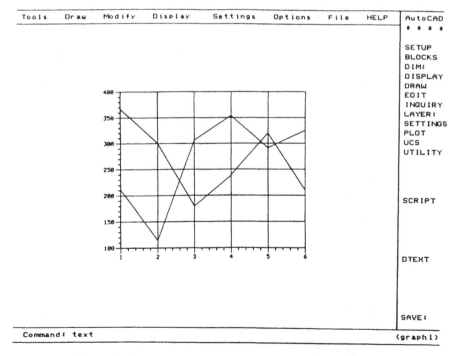

**Figure 9.1**   Simple line graph stored in GRAPH1.DWG.

(X) values and one for the vertical (Y) values. The lists will include the number of data values followed by the rest of the positions in the image. Each list will be called a *data array*. You may want to review AutoScript commands at this point to remember how to load data arrays.

The continuation of those procedures is discussed in this chapter. Using them, an engineer clearly depicts the concept; however, the presentation of the graph or chart can greatly influence its acceptance as outlined in this chapter. In this chapter we describe several special features that you can use to perform sequences of multiple charts or graphs and to create a professional-looking package.

## 9.3   Preview Packages

Autodesk provides a preview package technique called a *script* facility. This allows commands to be read from a text file. This feature allows an engineer to execute a predetermined sequence of commands that describe a graph as shown in Figure 9.2. As the

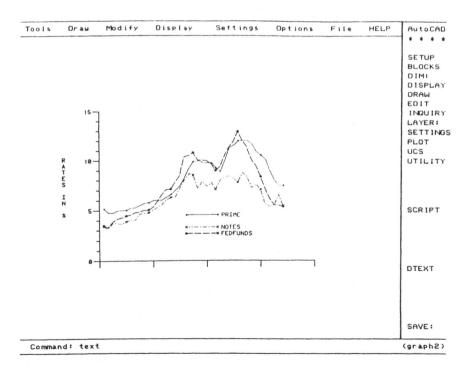

**Figure 9.2**   Line graph stored in GRAPH2.DWG.

designer, you can call these commands when you use a preview package (a special form of the ACAD command). You may also elect to run a preview file from the drawing editor by using the SCRIPT command. This type of graph is shown in Figure 9.3. Preview packages provide an easy way to create a continuously running display for chart and graph presentations such as Figure 9.4.

Preview files are created with AutoCAD text screens using a text editor. The file type must be .SCR, so that AutoCAD can locate the file. The AutoCAD UNDO feature considers a preview script to be a *data group* (shown in Figures 9.5 to 9.7), for which a single U command is used. Therefore, each line (command) in the created script file causes an entry to be made in the UNDO log. This can slow down review processing, and if you like, you can undo control none to turn off the UNDO before running the preview for clients. You should turn it back on by undo control all.

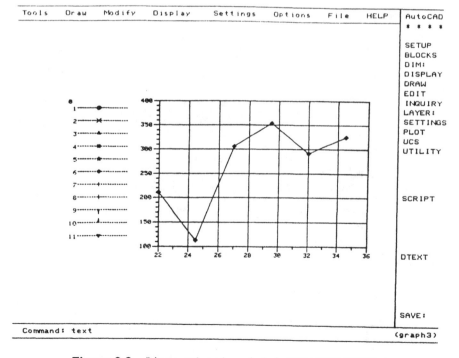

**Figure 9.3**   Line graph and symbols in GRAPH3.DWG.

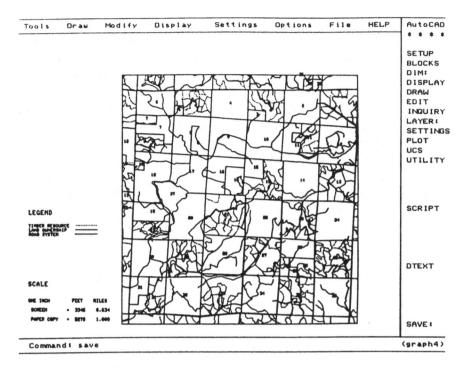

**Figure 9.4**   Chart showing timber resources in GRAPH4.DWG.

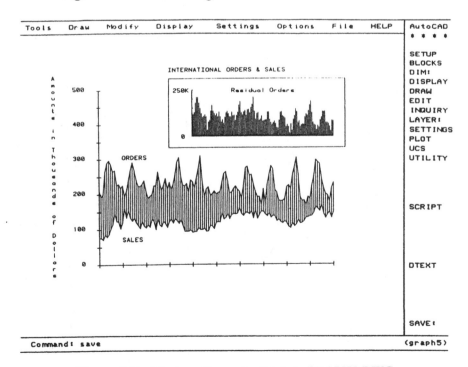

**Figure 9.5**   Display of two sets of data in GRAPH5.DWG.

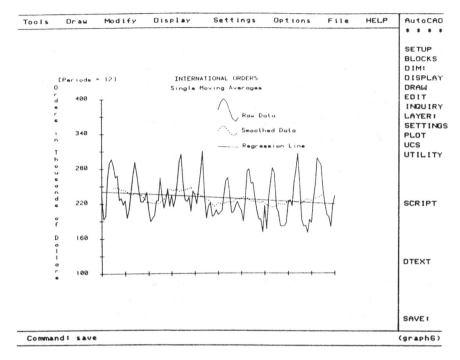

**Figure 9.6**   Display of three sets of data in GRAPHS.DWG.

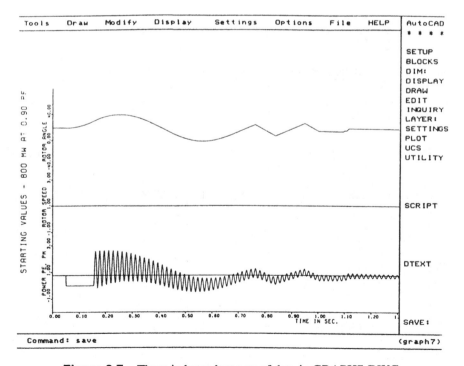

**Figure 9.7**   Three independent sets of data in GRAPH7.DWG.

## 9.4   Graph Preview When Loading

To call a graph preview when AutoCAD is first loaded, use the command C>acad graph1 preview, where graph1 is the drawing file created in Figure 9.8 and preview is the name for the script file created later in this chapter. This method of graph preview reads commands from GRAPH.DWG starting with the main menu prompts, so the first line of PREVIEW.SCR should select the desired task. The acad.msg sign-on message is skipped when PREVIEW.SCR is called. For example, suppose that every time you began a graph preview, you repeated all the early steps inside GRAPH1.DWG, which were

```
snap .5
grid
linetype scale 3
layer 0
color 0
```

A similar procedure is stored inside ACAD.DWG on your sample drawings diskette and is called a *prototype* drawing. This could be used to set up a graph preview, but a modified drawing file must be made each time a new graph is desired. This takes time;

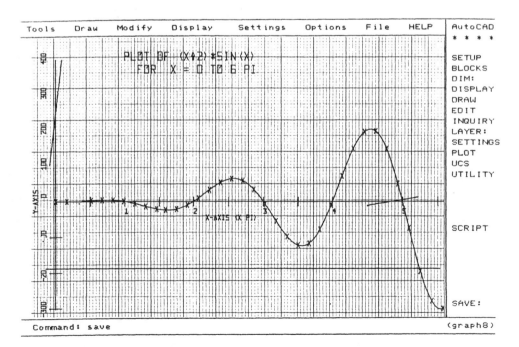

**Figure 9.8**   Equation graph in GRAPH8.DWG.

a quicker method is to do it with the following script, stored in a filed called SETUP.SCR.

```
1                  (create a new graph)
                   (blank line for default file name)
snap on            (turn on snap)
grid on            (turn on grid)
ltscale 3.0        (set scale/linetypes)
layer set 0        (current layer)
color red 0        (current color)
                   (ends layer sequence)
```

Now create a new graph called graph2 by C>acad graph2 setup. This sets the new graph name to graph2 (Figure 9.2) and begins reading commands from SETUP-SCR, which creates a series of graphs with the default name graph2, graph3 (Figure 9.3), graph4 (Figure 9.4), graph5 (Figure 9.5), ... and proceeds to issue the normal sequence of SETUP commands for each new graph in this chapter. At the end of a script file, the AutoCAD Command: prompt appears below the line on the bottom of the display screen and will await your first graph or chart procedure. As you become more familiar with the sequences of prompts issued by AutoCAD in Chapter 10, you will be able to create other useful loading script files.

## 9.5 Graph Preview ACAD Editor

To create a graph preview from within AutoCAD, use

```
Command: SCRIPT
Script file: graphs
```

The file type .SCR is assumed for graph8; you should not include it in your response. The sequence of commands stored in the graph preview file is executed, and the Command: prompt reappears. This assumes that a script file was created previously. Be careful in nesting script commands. For instance, if a SCRIPT command is read inside a script file (GRAPH8.SCR), that script file is terminated and the file named on the command becomes the new script file.

Several additional commands are available to make .SCR files more flexible. These are:

1. DELAY
2. RESUME
3. GRAPHSCR
4. TEXTSCR
5. QUIT Y and END
6. RSCRIPT
7. REGEN
8. SLIDE
9. MSLIDE
10. VSLIDE

## 9.6   DELAY Command

A graph preview as described above in the first three sections of this chapter is sort of a graphical flipchart. However, when alternative charts or graphs are placed back to back, the operations happen so quickly that it makes it difficult for reviewers to see what is taking place on the display screen. For example, if your GRAPH1.DWG and PREVIEW.SCR files draw lines and then erase them, the reviewers may not see them long enough to grasp their meaning. In addition, if several .DWG files are contained within a single .SCR file, the problem is even worse.

The DELAY command is provided to cause a sufficient pause between .SCR operations. It is used as follows:

```
Command: DELAY
Delay time in milliseconds: 5000
```

Five seconds of time is allowed for the pause. Naturally, the larger the number (5000 versus 8000), the longer the delay. The maximum delay time allowed is 32767, or about 30 seconds.

## 9.7   RESUME Command

To interrupt a running graph preview session, press Control C or the backspace key. The .SCR file interrupts at the end of the current command and allows you to issue drawing editor commands. If you later wish to return to the .SCR file at the point of interruption, enter

```
Command: RESUME
```

Any processing error from a .SCR file causes an interruption. If this occurs inside the drawing editor, use

```
Command: RESUME
```

to continue the script. If an editor command was in process when the error occurred, use

```
'RESUME
```

This is called a *transparent* command and does not require the prompt Command: to precede it.

## 9.8   GRAPHSCR and TEXTSCR Commands

Some AutoCAD commands (HELP, STATUS, etc.) flip automatically to the text display on a single-screen CAD workstation as used for this book. Although you can use the flip screen key to flip back to the graphics display manually, there is no way to include this key in a command script for graph preview. Therefore, two special commands are provided to permit .SCR files to flip between the graphics and text displays:

```
Command: GRAPHSCR
Command: TEXTSCR
```

These commands may also be used transparently as

```
'graphscr
'textscr
```
while another command is in progress.

## 9.9   QUIT Y and END Commands

For some graph previews it may be useful to have a .SCR file that reviews over and over, showing various aspects of a chart or graph. This can be done by calling the .SCR file when loading `acad` if the last command in the .SCR file is END or QUIT Y. These commands restart the .SCR file from the beginning of the main menu by C>acad graph10 preview, where graph10 is the default .DWG file and preview is the .SCR file. The `.scr` is assumed and should not be included in the call. The following is a simple example of this:

```
1                              (new drawing)
graph9                         (chart name)
snap on                        (turns snap on)
grid on                        (turns grid on)
elev 0                         (sets current elevation)
      1                        (sets current thickness)
                               (stops elevation commands)
line, 2,2 4,2, 4,4 2,4 c       (creates a prism)
delay 2000                     (pause 2 seconds)
move w 0,0 4,4 2,1             (moves chart 2 inchse right, 1 inch up)
                               (stops move command)
delay 1000                     (pause 1 second)
vpoint 1,-1,1                  (shows chart in pictorial)
delay 5000                     (pause 5 seconds)
quit y                         (recycle)
```

## 9.10   RSCRIPT and REGEN Commands

The RSCRIPT command is used to rewind and restart a .SCR file. This command must be the last command in the .SCR file and the file must be called from within AutoCAD as a drawing editor command:

```
Command: SCRIPT
Script file: review10
```

This command sequence is handled by the AutoCAD drawing editor; it does not cause the drawing editor to exit. Therefore, the script file should begin with drawing editor commands, not main menu responses (RSCRIPT is not understood by the main menu). Remove any END or QUIT Y commands at the end of the .SCR file and begin the file with `regen` instead of the `new  drawing` and `graph  name`.

## 9.11   SLIDE Commands

We are now ready to combine several graphs and charts into a single presentation. This is done with the slide commands MSLIDE and VSLIDE, which stand for "make a slide" and "view a slide." A slide is a separate file containing a snapshot of the graphics monitor. Whatever is on the display screen, a step in a graph construction or the entire graph, can be captured as a slide. In this manner the presentation is like looking at a slide show from a projector, but it is far more impressive and less time consuming than preparing 35mm slides of charts or graphs.

## 9.12   MSLIDE Command

Let us begin by preparing several demonstration slides. Locate the sample graphs and charts shown at the end of this chapter. Suppose that we select the first five. We begin the slide-making process by checking the first graph, SAMPLE.DWG as a current display, then enter

```
Command: MSLIDE
Slide file <sample>: (R)
```

The current drawing name <sample> is supplied by a default. Press the return and a file type of .SLD is created. A REDRAW operation takes place as the slide is being made, so that you can check the file contents.

You must repeat the process as

```
Command: MSLIDE
Slide file <sample2>:
Slide file <sample3>:
Slide file <sample4>:
Slide file <sample5>:
```

To make five separate slides.

## 9.13   VSLIDE Command

To view a slide, use the command

```
Command: VSLIDE
Slide file: sample
```

Do not include a .SLD extension in your response; it is assumed. If the specified file is found, it will be displayed for you. To view a series of slides, prepare a script file as follows:

```
vslide sample        (begin slide show)
vslide * sample2     (preloads second slide)
Delay 10000          (time delay 10 seconds)
vslide               (display sample 2)
vslide * sample3     (preloads third slide)
delay 10000
vslide               (displays sample 3)
vslide * sample4     (preloads fourth slide)
delay 10000
vslide               (displays sample 4)
vslide * sample5     (preloads fifth slide)
delay 10000
vslide               (displays sample 5)
delay 10000
rscript              (start sequence over)
```

## 9.14  Examples of Data Analysis

The eight examples in Figure 9.4 to 9.12 have been selected to illustrate some of the display techniques that can be used for CADD charts and graphs.

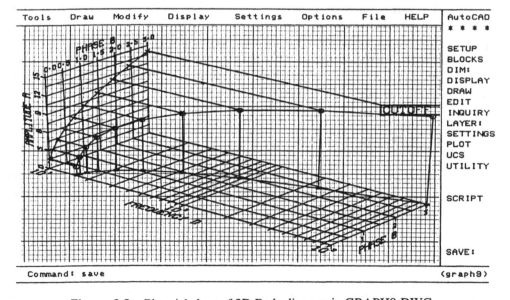

**Figure 9.9**  Pictorial chart of 3D Bode diagram in GRAPH9.DWG.

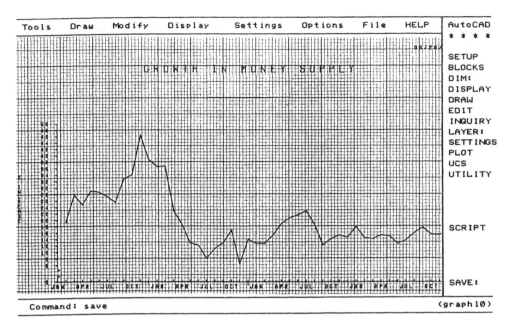

**Figure 9.10**   Data array stored in GRAPH10.DGW.

## 9.15   Linear Graphs

The majority of engineering graphs are plotted in rectangular coordinate format. This format is generally grided to form 1/20-inch square (Figures 9.8 to 9.10). Others are displayed in centimeters or in 1/10-, 1/8-, or ¼-inch squares. The larger grid makes the graph easier to read. Variables selected for the abscissa (X) and ordinate (Y) are chosen showing the independent variables as X and the dependent variables as Y. It is important to choose the correct scaling since this has an effect on the slope of the curve. The slope of the curve provides a visual impression of the degree of change in the dependent variable for a given increment of the independent variable. Always try to create the correct impression when using CADD.

## 9.16   Logarithmic Graphs

Logarithmic graphs may be created as shown in Figure 9.11; in fact, both linear and logarithmic are displayed within the same VDT image. You may compare the two types by the careful study of Figure 9.11.

## 9.17   Bar Graphs

Bar graphs may be created as shown in Figure 9.12. The AutoCAD HATCH routine is used to shade or fill the bars. Refer to Chapter 2 for a review of how to use HATCH.

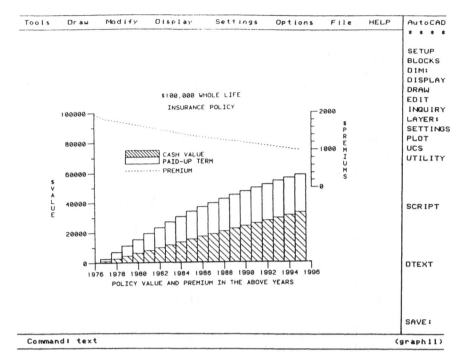

**Figure 9.11** Combination linear/logarithmic chart stored in GRAPH12.DWG.

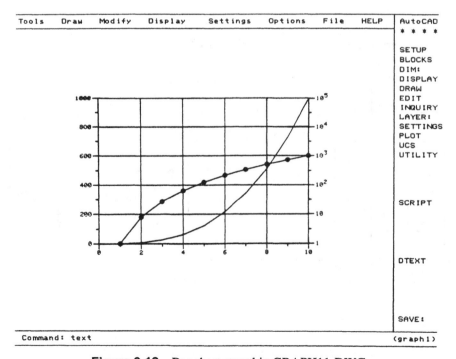

**Figure 9.12** Bar chart stored in GRAPH11.DWG.

## Exercises

Create the following displays.

1. Linear graph and store it as SAMPLE.DWG.

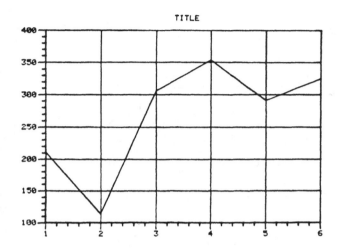

2. Linear graph and store it as SAMPLE2.DWG.

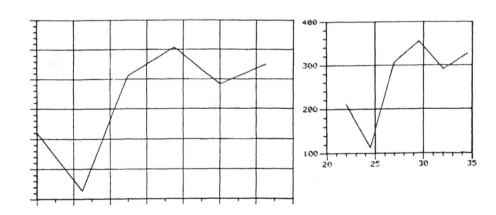

3. Graph and store it as SAMPLE3.DWG.

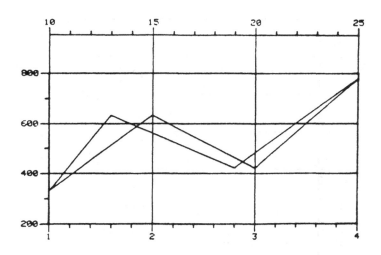

4. Graph and store it as SAMPLE4.DWG.

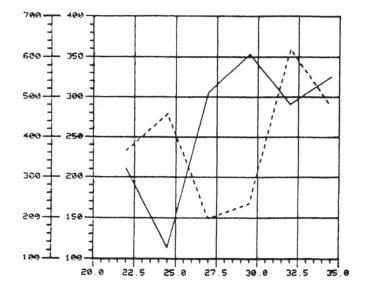

5.  Graph and store it as SAMPLE5.DWG.

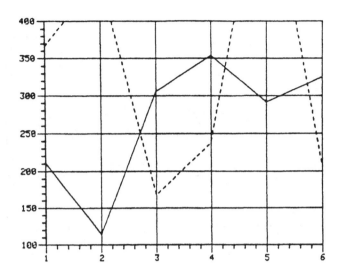

6.  Chart and store it as SAMPLE6.DWG.

|  |  | Screen coordinates | | | |
| Location | Value | XMIN | XMAX | YMIN | YMAX |
| --- | --- | --- | --- | --- | --- |
| STD (standard) | 1 | 150 | 900 | 150 | 700 |
| UPH (upper half) | 2 | 150 | 850 | 525 | 700 |
| LOH (lower half) | 3 | 150 | 850 | 150 | 325 |
| UL4 (upper left quarter) | 4 | 150 | 450 | 525 | 700 |
| UR4 (upper right quarter) | 5 | 650 | 950 | 525 | 700 |
| LL4 (lower left quarter) | 6 | 150 | 450 | 150 | 325 |
| LR4 (lower right quarter) | 7 | 650 | 950 | 150 | 325 |
| UL6 (upper left sixth) | 8 | 150 | 150 | 525 | 700 |
| UC6 (upper center sixth) | 9 | 475 | 475 | 525 | 700 |
| UR6 (upper right sixth) | 10 | 800 | 975 | 525 | 700 |
| LL6 (lower left sixth) | 11 | 150 | 325 | 150 | 325 |
| LC6 (lower center sixth) | 12 | 475 | 650 | 150 | 325 |
| LR6 (lower right sixth) | 13 | 800 | 975 | 150 | 325 |

7. Chart and store it as SAMPLE7.DWG.

| CONTROL | | HIGH X & Y GRAPHIC INPUT | | LOW X | | LOW Y | |
|---|---|---|---|---|---|---|---|
| NUL 0 | DLE 16 | SP 32 | ø 48 | @ 64 | P 80 | ` 96 | p 112 |
| SOH 1 | DC1 17 | ! 33 | 1 49 | A 65 | Q 81 | a 97 | q 113 |
| STX 2 | DC2 18 | " 34 | 2 50 | B 66 | R 82 | b 98 | r 114 |
| ETX 3 | DC3 19 | # 35 | 3 51 | C 67 | S 83 | c 99 | s 115 |
| EOT 4 | DC4 20 | $ 36 | 4 52 | D 68 | T 84 | d 100 | t 116 |
| ENQ 5 | NAK 21 | % 37 | 5 53 | E 69 | U 85 | e 101 | u 117 |
| ACK 6 | SYN 22 | & 38 | 6 54 | F 70 | V 86 | f 102 | v 118 |
| BEL 7 (BELL) | ETB 23 | ' 39 | 7 55 | G 71 | W 87 | g 103 | w 119 |
| BS 8 (BACK SPACE) | CAN 24 | ( 40 | 8 56 | H 72 | X 88 | h 104 | x 120 |
| HT 9 | EM 25 | ) 41 | 9 57 | I 73 | Y 89 | i 105 | y 121 |
| LF 10 (LINE FEED) | SUB 26 | * 42 | : 58 | J 74 | Z 90 | j 106 | z 122 |
| VT 11 | ESC 27 | + 43 | ; 59 | K 75 | [ 91 | k 107 | { 123 |
| FF 12 | FS 28 | , 44 | < 60 | L 76 | \ 92 | l 108 | ! 124 |
| CR 13 (RETURN) | GS 29 | - 45 | = 61 | M 77 | ] 93 | m 109 | } 125 |
| SO 14 | RS 30 | . 46 | > 62 | N 78 | ^ 94 | n 110 | ~ 126 |
| SI 15 | US 31 | / 47 | ? 63 | O 79 | — 95 | o 111 | 127 RUBOUT (DEL) |

8. Logarithmic graph and store as SAMPLE8.DWG.

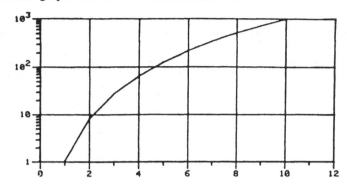

9. Bar graph and store as SAMPLE9.DGW.

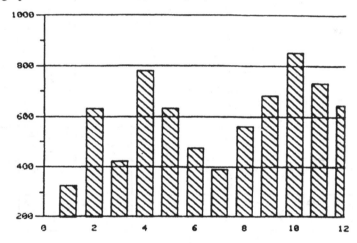

10. Hatch patterns and store as SAMPLE10.DWG.

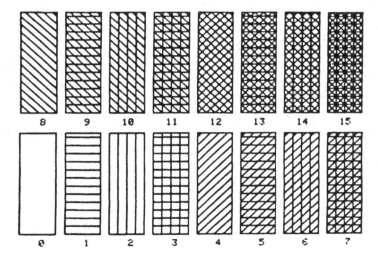

# 10

# Sample Programs and User Problems

In the first nine chapters, computer-aided graphics and design have been categorized as human–machine communication. What goes on inside the workstation between a human being's input and the machine's output is called *processing*. This takes place according to the software (Autodesk programs) and user-produced programs placed in the graphics workstation. The graphics workstation receives graphic input and creates graphic output as described throughout this book. In summary, the earlier chapters considered how a person handles graphic information so that the workstation can process the following files:

1. Drawing  < file.dwg >
2. Sketch  < file.skd >
3. Menus  < file.mnu >
4. Script  < file.scr >
5. Interchange between Autodesk  < file.dxf >
6. Photographs (binary)  < file.dxb)
7. IGES  < file.igs >

## 10.1   User Applications

A user of this book will learn how to extend the basic Autodesk software capabilities and use the extensions for special applications. In this chapter we teach you how to design your own menus and libraries to complement those demonstrated in the first nine chapters. Use of multiple file directories and the format of the HELP text file are also discussed in this chapter. Autodesk makes full use of the tree-structured file directories discussed in Chapter 3. If you do not remember DOS (or your operating system) that well, you can simply place all Autodesk program files and auxiliary files (menus, text font files, HELP file) in the current working directory and keep your drawing files there as well.

   If you would like to maintain several directories of drawings but only one copy of the Autodesk directory, that is also possible. Simply place the entire contents of the current Autodesk release disks in a directory that is on your operating system. Then, whether or not you make that directory the current directory when you execute Autodesk, all the necessary items will be available. For instance, if you have used the DOS command

```
drive>path C: .bin;C: .progs
```

you can place the Autodesk files in either of two directories (BIN or PROGS), but do not divide the files between the two. Since both directories are on the DOS search path, DOS and Autodesk will be able to find the necessary files for proper operation. You can create as many directories as you like. Suppose that you had a different directory for each student assignment or commercial client with a subdirectory for each week of the semester. The structure and meaning of your directories is up to you. When you want to work on a drawing in a particular directory, you can make that directory current and then call Autodesk.

```
drive> cd .schema .week1
drive> acad
```

If you would like, you can edit a drawing without making its directory the current directory. Whenever Autodesk prompts you for a file name, you can reply with a simple name, a name preceded with a drive letter, or a full path name, including directory names.

```
parts .handle
```

If you enter a file name with neither drive nor directory prefixes, Autodesk assumes that you mean a file in the current directory.


## 10.2   Application Menus

An application menu is simply a text file of the type .MNU that contains Autodesk command strings. Sections of the file can be connected to different menu devices, such as the screen menus shown in earlier chapters. To construct a menu, use script for each menu item (command, parameter, or sequences). A simple menu might look as follows:

```
;script file for sample menu
  line
  zoom A
  zoom W
  GRID ON
  GRID OFF
  GRID .1
  [ FSNAP] 0.001
  [ CSNAP] 0.1
  [ DONE] end
  [ GIVE UP] quit
  [ ADDIR] save;tx
```

Wuen you view the menu, only eight characters will appear in each line, as follows:

```
| line
| zoom A
| zoom B
| GRID ON
| GRID OFF
| FSNAP
| CSNAP
| DONE
| GIVE UP
| ADDIR;tx
```

When you select any of the following items from the menu, Autodesk treats it as though you had typed it directly after the Command: in the prompt area. Notice the use of square brackets to produce the menu items FSNAP, CSNAP, DONE, GIVE UP, and ADDIR. These are the labels only for the commands of SNAP 0.001 and SNAP 0.1, quit and save. It might be useful to think of these as FINE SNAP, COARSE SNAP, DRAWING END, and QUIT Y, and add them to your drawing directory.

A menu file can also be broken into several sections which are identified by section labels. Each section belongs to a different workstation item, as described earlier. The sections are entered in a menu file.

```
;script file for sample menu2.
  ***SCREEN       (side screen menu area)
  ***TABLET 1     (first tablet area)
  ***TABLET 2     (second tablet area)
  ***TABLET 3     (third area)
  ***TABLET 4     (fourth area)
```

These labels appear in a .MNU file.

```
***SCREEN
[ INFO] help
[ BYE] quit y
```

```
***TABLET 1
[RECT] pline
[CIRCL] circle
[WALL] trace
***TABLET2
block
layer
***TABLET3
backspace
<
***TABLET4
TEXT
DIM1
EDIT
OSNAP
PLOT
```

## 10.3 Submenus

A menu section can be very large, containing many more items than there are screen locations to place them. A submenu is a collection of smaller groups of menu items within a menu.

```
**string
```

where STRING is a name up to 31 characters long. All submenu names within a .MNU file must be unique. Menu items that follow a **STRING belong to that submenu.

```
;script file for menu3
  **floorplan
  [walls] trace
  [windows] pline
  [doors] arc;line
  **elevation
  [brick] hatch
  [roof] trace
  [vent] circle
```

Floorplan is a submenu name and contains three elements (walls, windows, and doors). Additional items can be added up to the limit of the screen menu area or the tablet location. Elevation is a submenu name and also contains three elements. When **STRING is active, its list of items replaces those of the previous screen menu, starting at the top and continuing through the list. You may want to skip over the top, down the order.

```
**string n
```

where n is the starting position in the list. For example, n = 4 would begin in the fourth position, with the first three positions unchanged from the previous submenu shown.

In addition, you may place the submenu in any of four locations.

;script file for sample menu.

```
$S  = string        (means screen)
$T1 = string        (means tablet area 1)
$T2 = string        (means tablet area 2)
$T3 = string        (means tablet area 3)
$T4 = string        (means tablet area 4)
```

## 10.4  Adding Linetypes

The Autodesk software includes a library of standard linetypes in the file acad.lin. You may locate and view these. As you can see, not all drafting or design linetypes are included, and you will want to modify or create your own.

To create or modify a linetype definition, enter the linetype command and choose the Create option.

```
Command: LINETYPE
?/Create/Load/Set: C
```

Autodesk prompts:

```
Name of linetype to create:
File storage lintype <default>:
```

Respond with the name of the linetype you wish to create and the name of the library file in which you will store its definition. Do not include a file type .LIN after the name; this is assumed. If you use any of the names used by Autodesk, the prompt

```
Name already exists in this file.
Overwrite (Y/N)<N>?
```

will appear. If you answer N, a new linetype name and file name is requested. If you answer Y, the current definition will be destroyed and replaced with a new definition.

```
Descriptive text:
Enter pattern (on next line):
A, .5,-.5,.5,-.5,.5,-.5,.5
```

This will produce a linetype like

A response to A of 1,-.5,1,-.5,1 will produce

and a response of .5,-.25,0,-.25,1 will produce

You will have noticed that linetypes are created with a pen up (minus numbers) or pen down (positive numbers). The numbers represent drawing units on the screen. If 1 unit equals 1 inch, the linetypes can be measured with a common ruler. Also notice that a pen value of zero creates a dot.

## 10.5   Hatch Patterns

The hatch patterns are stored in the file ACAD.PAT. You can locate this file and read it or add to it if you like. Each of the hatch patterns begins with a header line (*name, description) and one or more lines. For example, a pattern called section could be added.

```
;script file additional lines
   *section
   45,0,0,0,0,.125;tx
```

This simple pattern would draw lines at a 45° angle beginning at the lower left-hand corner of the hatch window, continuing to the upper right-hand corner at a line spacing of 1/8 of an inch. The complete list of hatch patterns available, 40 in all, is as follows:

| | | | |
|---|---|---|---|
| angle | cross | honey | stars |
| ansi131 | dash | hound | steel |
| ansi32 | dolmit | insul | swamp |
| ansi34 | dots | sacncr | trans |
| ansi38 | earth | mudst | triang |
| box | escher | net | zigzag |
| brass | flex | net3 | line |
| brick | grass | plast | net |
| clay | grate | plasti | ansi37 |
| cork | stars | square | null |

## 10.6   Text Fonts

In this section we describe how to define font files for text or drawing symbols. Shapes are described using formatted text in the file acad.shp. The output of such a file can be seen by looking at the file; here the standard text fonts of TXT, SIMPLEX, COMPLEX, and ITALIC are shown. To modify these or create a new text font, select task 7 from the main Autodesk menu. You will remember from Chapter 3 that this task was designed to compile a shape file into a format that was digested more rapidly by the LOAD or STYLE command of Autodesk. When you select task 7, Autodesk prompts

```
Enter NAME of shape file:
```

A shape file description (list of commands) should exist at this point so that Autodesk can compile the file EXAMPLE.SHP. Do not include the .SHP when you enter the name after the prompt. The compilation will take a few seconds, and then Autodesk will respond

```
Compilation successful.
Output file contains 47 bytes.
```

Notice that a compiled file is called EXAMPLE.SHX and a file with shape commands is called EXAMPLE.SHP.

## 10.7 Shape Files

As noted in Section 10.6, shape descriptions have a file of .SHP. Autodesk comes with two sample shape files (pc.shx and es.shx). The first is for printed circuit layout, and the second is for electronic schematics. Examining these files will help you understand the creation of shape files.

In general, every shape in a file must have a unique number between 1 and 255. *Note:* Text fonts require specific numbers corresponding to the value of each character in the ASCII data (see the ASCII chart in Chapter 9, Exercise 7). Other shapes can be assigned whatever numbers you like. Each shape also has a header line.

```
*shp#,bytes,name
```

when shp# is any number between 1 and 255, bytes is the number of data bytes required to describe the shape (string length limit 2000), and name is the file label (example above).

## 10.8 HELP File

The HELP file inside Autodesk is kept in ACAD.HLP. This is a standard text file and can be edited to suit your needs. As you work with Autodesk you will find yourself using the HELP command to better understand many of the items in this book. After many months of use, the HELP file will seem unusually long, boring, or just not very useful because you have found certain shortcuts in your daily work. These shortcuts can be passed along to co-workers and fellow students by editing (adding to or subtracting from) ACAD.HLP.

## 10.9 Drawing Interchange Files

In this section we describe the DXF (drawing interchange files) format and the commands provided to use these files. Autodesk can be used by itself as a complete design and drawing editor as shown in Chapters 3 and 4. In some applications, other programs developed on the workstation must examine drawings created by Autodesk software packages as listed in Chapter 1. Drawing files may be transported between Autodesk software packages through the DXF format.

Since our database is stored in a very compact format, it is hard for user programs to read directly. DXF files are standard ASCII text files. They can therefore be translated to the formats of other packages submitted to other programs for specialized analysis. You create a DXF from an existing drawing inside Autodesk software. The name of the DXF file is the name given to the drawing currently in operation. Let us say that we are working inside a file CAT.DWG. When the DXFOUT command is executed, a file CAT.DXF is created.

A DXF format can be converted into a .DWG file by entering Autodesk and creating a new drawing space from the main menu.

```
Command: DXFIN File Name:
```

Enter the DXF file name without the extension .DXF.

Of course, the conversion can be made outside Autodesk as well. Figure 10.1 is an example of a BASIC program that reads a DXF file and extracts all the line entities from the drawing. It prints the end points of these lines on the screen. As a learning exercise, you might want to try entering this program into your workstation, running it on a DXF file from one of your drawings completed in Chapter 9, then enhancing it to print the graph of chart.

Writing a program that constructs a DXF file is more difficult because you must maintain consistency within the drawing in order for Autodesk to find it acceptable. Figure 10.2 is a program that constructs a DXF file representing a polygon with a specified number of sides, leftmost origin point, and side length.

## 10.10   Binary Drawing Interchange

A DXB (drawing interchange binary) is a much more compact file format. You may use this format to transport digital camera images into Autodesk software. To load a DXB file produced by a camera, enter

```
Command: DXBIN
DXB file:
```

Enter the name of the file you wish to load from the camera scan. Do not include a file type DXB; this is assumed. See Chapter 5 for more information on camera inputs for pictorial representation.

## 10.11   IGES Files

Initial graphics exchange standard (IGES) files can be used to instruct Autodesk to read and write IGES format files. You can generate an IGES file from an existing drawing.

```
Command: IGESOUT
File name:
```

Once this has been done, the drawing default name is used to produce a .IGS file. When you wish to use an IGES file from someone else:

```
1000 REM
1010 REM Extract lines from DXF file
1020 REM
1030 LINE INPUT "DXF file name: "; A$
1040 A$=A$+".dxf"
1050 OPEN "i",1,A$
1060 REM
1070 REM Ignore until section start encountered
1080 REM
1090 GOSUB 1320
1100 IF G% <> 0 THEN 1090
1110 IF S$ <> "SECTION" THEN 1090
1120 GOSUB 1320
1130 REM
1140 REM Skip unless ENTITIES section
1150 REM
1160 IF S$ <> "ENTITIES" THEN 1090
1170 REM
1180 REM Scan until end of section processing LINEs
1190 REM
1200 GOSUB 1320
1210 IF G% = 0 AND S$="ENDSEC" THEN STOP
1220 IF G%=0 AND S$="LINE" THEN GOSUB 1270 : GOTO 1210
1230 GOTO 1200
1240 REM
1250 REM Accumulate LINE entity groups
1260 REM
1270 GOSUB 1320
1280 IF G%=10 THEN X1=X : Y1=Y
1290 IF G%=11 THEN X2=X : Y2=Y
1300 IF G%=0 THEN PRINT "Line from (";X1;",";Y1;
     ") to (";X2;",";Y2;")" : RETURN
1310 GOTO 1270
1320 REM
1330 REM Read group code and following value
1340 REM
1350 INPUT #1, G%
1360 IF G% < 10 THEN LINE INPUT #1, S$ : RETURN
1370 IF G% >= 30 AND G% <= 49 THEN INPUT #1, V : RETURN
1380 IF G% >= 50 AND G% <= 59 THEN INPUT #1, A : RETURN
1390 IF G% >= 60 AND G% <= 69 THEN INPUT #1, P% : RETURN
1400 IF G% >= 70 AND G% <= 79 THEN INPUT #1, F% : RETURN
1410 IF G% >=20 THEN PRINT "Invalid group code ";G% : STOP
1420 INPUT #1,X
1430 INPUT #1,G1%
1440 IF G1% <> (G%+10) THEN PRINT "Invalid Y coord code ";
     G1% : STOP
1450 INPUT #1,Y
1460 RETURN
```

**Figure 10.1** Program to read DXE. (Courtesy DLR Associates.)

```
1000 REM
1010 REM Polygon generator
1020 REM
1030 LINE INPUT "Drawing (DXF) file name: "; A$
1040 OPEN "o",1,A$+".dxf"
1050 PRINT #1,0
1060 PRINT #1,"SECTION"
1070 PRINT #1,2
1080 PRINT #1,"ENTITIES"
1090 PI=ATN(1)*4
1100 INPUT "Number of sides for polygon: ";S%
1110 INPUT "Starting point (X,Y): ";X,Y
1120 INPUT "Polygon side: ";D
1130 A1=(2*PI)/S%
1140 A=PI/2
1150 FOR I%=1 TO S%
1160 PRINT #1,0
1170 PRINT #1,"LINE"
1180 PRINT #1,8
1190 PRINT #1,"0"
1200 PRINT #1,10
1210 PRINT #1,X
1220 PRINT #1,20
1230 PRINT #1,Y
1240 NX=D*COS(A)+X
1250 NY=D*SIN(A)+Y
1260 PRINT #1,11
1270 PRINT #1,NX
1280 PRINT #1,21
1290 PRINT #1,NY
1300 X=NX
1310 Y=NY
1320 A=A+A1
1330 NEXT I%
1340 PRINT #1,0
1350 PRINT #1,"ENDSEC"
1360 PRINT #1,0
1370 PRINT #1,"EOF"
1380 CLOSE 1
```

**Figure 10.2**   Program to generate DXF. (Courtesy DLR Associates).

```
Command: IGESIN
File name:
```

Enter the name of the file to be loaded.


## 10.12   Case Studies

Each of the case studies presented below is stated with reference to certain information
contained in the first nine chapters. Following this description, a discussion of the problem containing the drawing file is presented. By using this format, the material presented
in the book is summarized in case study form. This format replaces the usual exercises
used in earlier chapters.

### 10.12.1 Automated Title Block

**Statement of the problem.** Modify the drawing files shown in Chapter 1 so that changes in sheet sizes can be made. Make the changes necessary so that a size A, B, or C sheet border and title strip can be selected.

**Discussion.** Drawing files called blocks are prepared so that the user may simplify the display process. A tile block may be added to a new drawing file or an old one by merging the block name TITLEA into the file for a size A sheet format, as shown in Figure 10.3.

### 10.12.2 Digitizing Problem

**Statement of the problem.** Digitize a simple object as described in Chapter 2. Use the simple object as a test for the commands GRID, SNAP, and SKETCH. Use the subcommand contained within SKETCH and the screen grid to create a simple drawing.

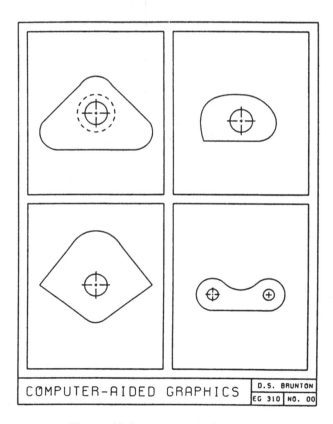

**Figure 10.3** Automated title block.

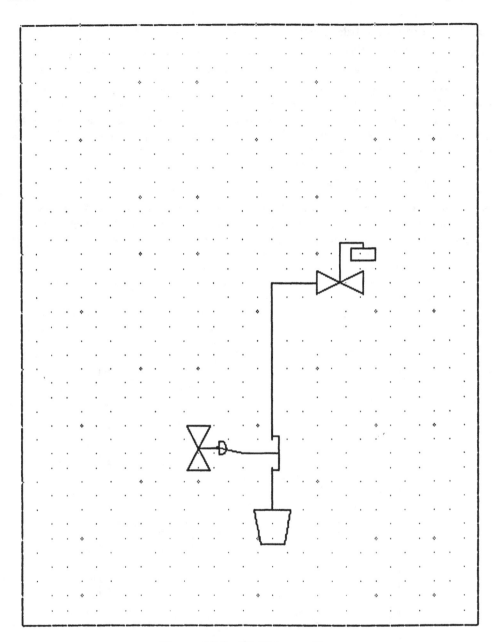

**Figure 10.4**  Digitizing problem.

**Discussion**. The technique of describing a graphic shape by grid locations is called *digitizing*. Examples from Chapter 2 can be digitized by counting grid locations in the horizontal and vertical directions and using a single Autodesk command: SKETCH as shown in Figure 10.4.

### 10.12.3   Geometric Constructions

**Statement of the problem**. Choose any of the progressive student exercise files from Chapter 3 and arrange an output as shown in Figure 10.5. Merge the proper-sized title block.

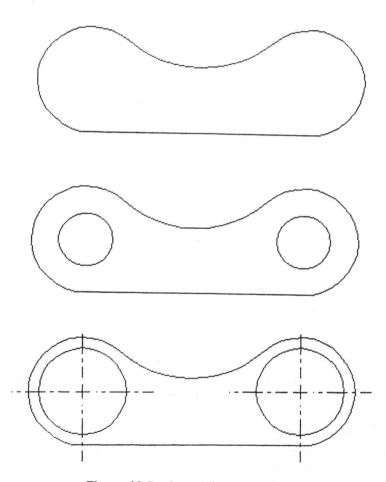

**Figure 10.5**   Geometric constructions.

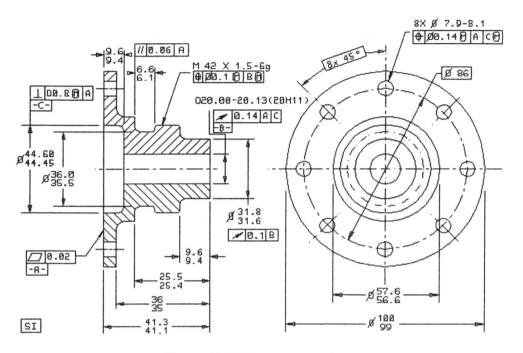

**Figure 10.6**   Piece part selection.

**Discussion.**   You will use the Autodesk commands described in Chapter 3 to form shape descriptions that will replace the laborious SKETCH procedures of Case Study 2.

### 10.12.4   Piece Part Selection

**Statement of the problem.**   Select any of the exercises at the end of Chapter 4 and arrange a sheet layout as shown in Figure 10.6.

**Discussion.**   Case studies 1, 2, and 3 work admirably for drawings composed exclusively of straight lines, circles, and discrete points. These CADD techniques require painstaking effort on the part of the workstation operator. Case Study 4 will be developed to practice dimensioning patterns to be described in compact formats.

### 10.12.5   Autodesk Symbol Library

**Statement of the problem.**   A symbol library for Autodesk software exists for your use. Prepare a simple diagram as shown in Figure 10.7.

**Discussion.**   Study the example symbol library shown on p. 253.

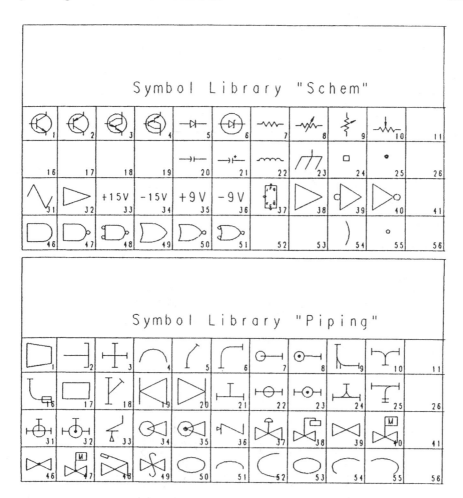

### 10.12.6 Electronics Circuit Analysis

**Statement of the problem.** Case study 5 can be used in the creation of an electronics schematic as shown in Figure 10.8.

**Discussion.** Lines used to connect the symbols can be butted directly to the connection node of each symbol with the command OSNAP. The symbols are arranged according to an engineer's sketch or written description.

### 10.12.7 Computer Modeling Techniques

**Statement of the problem.** Prepare a .DWG file that will produce the profile of Figure 10.9.

**Discussion.** Four equations will be based in the solution: III is a straight line tangent at point –7 on the X axis, II is a parabola from the –7 to a +5 on the Y axis, I is a circle with a radius of 10 units, and IV is a straight-line segment tangent to the circle at the X axis.

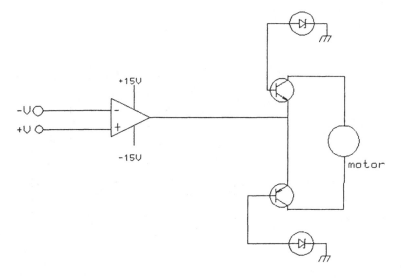

**Figure 10.7**  Simple diagram.

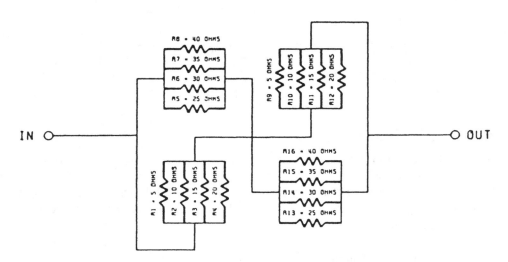

IN O                                                                    O OUT

**Figure 10.8**  Electronic circuit analysis.

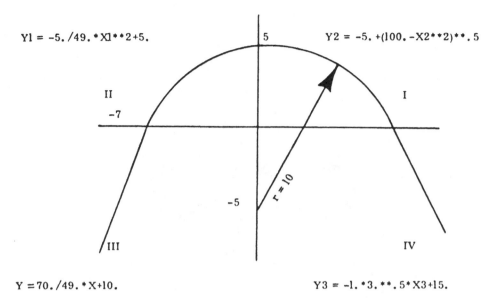

Yl = -5./49.*Xl**2+5.        |5        Y2 = -5.+(100.-X2**2)**.5

Y = 70./49.*X+10.                    Y3 = -1.*3.**.5*X3+15.

**Figure 10.9**   Computer modeling techniques.

### 10.12.8  Computerized Path Specification

**Statement of the problem.**   Use Figure 10.10 as an example of path specification. You may use Case Study 7 profile shape if desired, or you may create a new one.
**Discussion.**   Use the display techniques from Chapter 5 and the design skills from Chapters 6 to 8.

### 10.12.9  Part Animation Studies

**Statement of the problem.**   The application programming shown in Chapter 9 to make and show a slide may be used to display a part.
**Discussion.**   Use Figure 10.11 as an example of several separate slides that are superimposed one on the other. Prepare a script file to display up to 100 animation positions for the part chosen.

### 10.12.10  Surface Descriptions

**Statement of the problem.**   Using the display techniques from Chapter 5, select one of the surface display teachniques shown in Figure 5.17 and produce a display similar to Figure 10.12.
**Discussion.**   Refer to Chapter 5 for the descriptions of display surfaces. You may want to try different techniques (cubic, Bezier, or linear interpolation) on the same database.

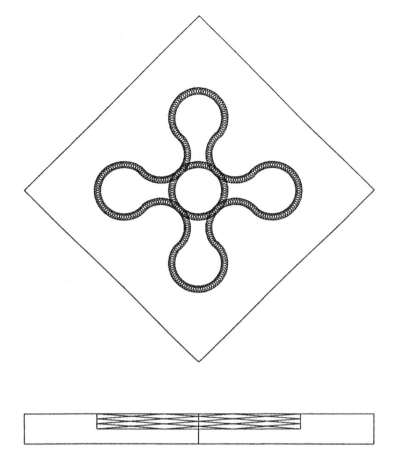

**Figure 10.10**   Path specification.

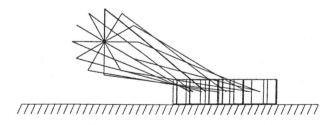

**Figure 10.11**   Path animation.

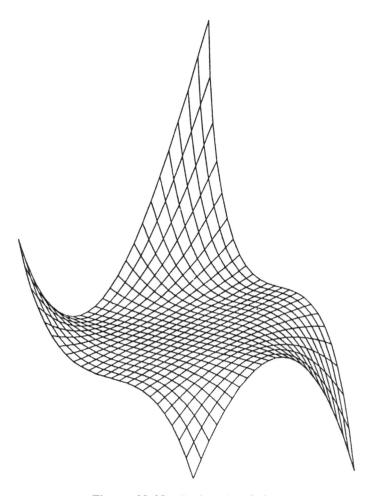

**Figure 10.12** Surface description.

# Index

Printed in the United States
by Baker & Taylor Publisher Services